A HALO PUBLISHING INTERNATIONAL ANTHOLOGY

SHATTERED SILENCE

STORIES OF LOSS AND HEALING

A HALO PUBLISHING INTERNATIONAL ANTHOLOGY

SHATTERED SILENCE

STORIES OF LOSS AND HEALING

Halo Publishing International
7550 WIH-10 #800, PMB 2069,
San Antonio, TX 78229

First Edition, April 2024
ISBN: 978-1-63765-550-4
Library of Congress Control Number: 2023924709

Halo Publishing International is a self-publishing company that publishes adult fiction and non-fiction, children's literature, self-help, spiritual, and faith-based books. We continually strive to help authors reach their publishing goals and provide many different services that help them do so. We do not publish books that are deemed to be politically, religiously, or socially disrespectful, or books that are sexually provocative, including erotica. Halo reserves the right to refuse publication of any manuscript if it is deemed not to be in line with our principles. Do you have a book idea you would like us to consider publishing? Please visit www.halopublishing.com for more information.

Acknowledgements

We extend our heartfelt gratitude to every individual
who has made a contribution to this book

Diane Lopes

Irene S. Roth

Angela Gilson

Anapaula Corral

Monica Septimio

Dave Grunenwald

Lisa Michelle Umina

Conrad M. Gonzales

Fran Walsh Ward, PhD

Dr. Carol Leibovich-Mankes

Contents

Our Authors

Introduction

Fran Walsh Ward, PhD

*G*rief is a relentless terrorist that abducts human beings and transforms them into zombie shadows of their former selves. Grief does not discriminate. It can overcome universally; or it can annihilate the body, mind, and spirit of an individual. Grief can ravage a community, a continent, or the whole world in one fell swoop. The invader's grasp is ubiquitous. No one is safe from the clutches of grief.

Although intertwined, grief and grieving are different. *Grief* is a natural *emotion* in reaction to experiencing loss. *Grieving* is the mourning *process* following the loss.

Usually manifesting first in physical form, such as crying, grief is felt in the solar plexus and migrates up the chest and through the brain to evoke memories and also a need for the bereaved to connect with others. Triggered by any kind of loss, grief can be the worst experience in a person's life.

***

This first chapter of the anthology *Shattered Silence: Stories of Loss and Healing* is a reflection of universal human conditions garnered along my path as a teacher, writer, peace advocate, and participant in rituals and practices of many faiths and cultures.

***

Grief is a thief. No person or culture can escape its criminal nature. It steals the breath. Lungs control the flow of energy in a body. Crying, convulsive gasps of despair, and holding in the breath decrease oxygen, the life force that fuels humans. Grief is emotion harbored in the lungs and large intestine. Emotional blockage from not letting go of grief can interfere with the in-and-out action of the lungs and with normal physical elimination functions, both of which leave a person feeling drained of energy.

Any kind of loss can trigger feelings of depression. Other common visible symptoms of grief are strong feelings of sadness or sorrow, lack of focus, inability to trust, loss of purpose in living, constant thoughts of what was lost, and denial of the loss.

Everyone thinks that his own grief and pain are the worst. The Holmes-Rahe Life Stress Inventory assigns numeric values to major life factors, but numbers cannot reflect the hurt inside. No one's grief should be marginalized (see the website stress.org for the inventory to score your own recent life stress). Our innate sense of compassion guides us to sympathize with all unspeakable losses that members of our family of man have suffered. We are *all* connected. The Stress Inventory rates the death of a spouse as the greatest life stressor (a divorce and a jail term rank equally high). Everywhere in the world, spouses are grieving lost loves. Half of all Americans report having lost a loved one in the last three years.

***

My dear friend is one of those suffering. She documented her husband's heartbreaking health decline. It is unimaginable how she mustered her strength to monitor his changes, administer treatments, comfort him, and post painful-to-read updates for our friends. Following his death, we sympathized as she mourned his loss, but we could not make her pain go away. No one could. Nothing can. She is adjusting to an empty world without him. Life will never be the same. She has memories, but she does not have him. We grieve for her and trust that she can cope. It will take time, patience, and forgoing expectations for her to move on without him; but the hope is that she can and she will.

I met a widow in a different situation in a taverna near Athens, Greece. Dressed in black, she was sitting at the exit by the cash register. She was the personification of sadness. Feeling grief for her lamented husband was the life she chose. Her grief, known as perpetual grief, indicates an inability or lack of desire to step forward and leave the past in the past. For someone experiencing inability to progress through the stages to approach healing, therapy can help.

***

Elizabeth Kübler-Ross, in 1969, proposed the death-adjustment pattern of five stages of grief: denial, anger, bargaining, depression, and acceptance. Since then, alternative paradigms for experiencing death and grief have been introduced stressing that the process is not necessarily linear and that stages can be experienced simultaneously and without time limits. "Shock and disbelief" have replaced the term denial, and "searching and yearning" attempt to explain one's new reality. Each person grieves in his own way in order to heal and be able to give and receive love.

***

The widow I met in Greece was not alone in the depths of her anguish. Her grief is magnified by 6,000 times in

Vrindavan, India, the City of Widows. Since the sixteenth century when a widow was expected to immolate herself on her husband's funeral pyre, women have escaped to Vrindavan. The horrific self-sacrificial practice is now outlawed, but draconian laws in India have not improved sufficiently to grant property rights to castaway widows to alleviate their homeless condition.

Many of these widows in India are illiterate and have been in arranged marriages since they were fourteen years old. Banished by the family of the deceased, they feel unworthy of love or life. Widowhood can mean disaster for forty million widows each year who have been purged from their husbands' patriarchal family homes. They flock to Vrindavan, India. Barefoot and wearing white saris to symbolize that all color has been leached from their lives, they swarm the dirt streets by the thousands and spend their remaining days praying, singing devotional songs in temples and ashrams, and begging from tourists visiting the holy city of the childhood home of the Hindu Lord Krishna, the god of compassion, protection, and love. These widows seek comfort in their faith.

**

In a family, there's another death that is universally tragic. The death of any child is catastrophic.

Grief takes life hostage when it abducts a child. The supreme artistic example of this can be seen in *La Pietà*, the masterpiece by Michelangelo, who is also known as the Divine One. This sculpture imbued one solid piece of marble with all the anguish of a mother who has lost her child. It is located in St. Peter's Basilica at the Vatican in Rome, and it depicts the Blessed Virgin Mary cradling the body of her slain son, Jesus Christ, following His descent from the cross. *La Pietà* is rich in meaning and emotion, and it is the only work of art Michelangelo ever signed.

The name of this sculpture is said to come from the Italian word for *pity* and the Latin word for *piety*. Emotion flows from the artist through the statue to the visitors in the Vatican who observe, kneel, weep, wail, and express personal and religious emotions towards Mother, Son, and mankind.

When I visited the Vatican (which is sacred but public), it felt as if it were an invasion of privacy to bear witness to the torment in one mother's torturous voice as it wrenched everyone's hearts and filled the cavernous space with woe.

I believe that the Holmes-Rahe Stress Inventory neglects to include the loss of a child as an unparalleled pain. Many individuals, speaking from personal experience, say that death of a child is the greatest pain imaginable.

Our hearts ache when we learn of the death of any child. Parents are inconsolable when a child is ripped away from childhood under any circumstances. Whether the cause was a medical condition, an accident, a natural disaster, or any other reason, the pain is universal. It is palpable. We feel it, and we empathize. When the death occurs under unnatural circumstances, grief is compounded.

Parents grieve equally, but male grief and female grief are often expressed differently. They are both intense, but women can often emote and express themselves. When a friend's toddler niece died of meningitis, her uncle expressed anger, hurt, suffering, anguish, and torment. Men are steam kettles that can bubble and boil over. There is no right way or wrong way for anyone to express emotion. When grief takes possession of a person, pressure must be released, or confusion can prevail, regardless of the cause of the loss.

***

Grieving can begin even while someone who will be mourned is still alive. Anticipatory grief is a reaction to an expected death. Caregivers can experience anticipatory grief for an individual with a terminal illness and might begin to envision life without that person. Someone can also experience grief following a job layoff (such as occurred during the coronavirus pandemic), a divorce, or a medical diagnosis.

***

I experienced anticipatory grief and grieving while I was in Vietnam. I visited a leprosy hospital near Ho Chi Minh City (formerly Saigon, the South Vietnamese capital during the Vietnam War). The hospital was filled with crying and grieving patients, parents, and visitors. A little-boy patient was lying on the floor in the corridor. He was blue—not from air temperature or lack of oxygen. His exposed skin was as bright a blue as that of members of the Blue Man Group performers. I did not express the shock that I felt when I saw him. When he waved his little hand at me, I smiled and waved back.

I was led from room to room by hospital personnel. I waved hello to every patient. I was happy to see patients of all ages smile and wave back. I don't know if all visitors to that hospital are taken to see the patients, but I felt that grief was suspended for a time during my unannounced visit as an ordinary American tourist.

Only after my visit did I read that leprosy (now called Hansen's disease) is still endemic in some areas of the world, including Southeast Asia. As I left the hospital, I asked why the boy was blue. He had been painted blue as his personal invitation to the Hindu Boy God, Lord Krishna (one of the most popular and revered Hindu deities, the god of protection, compassion, tenderness, and love, whose birthplace is Vrindavan, the City of Widows). Blue gods have a blue aura. Blue is the color that represents anything that is vast and beyond perception, like the ocean or the sky. So much seems to be beyond our perception, such as grieving and healing.

***

Natural disasters have also provided us common terrors, as well as opportunities for unification beyond our perception. Climate change has shown us a side of Mother Nature that we never imagined in our wildest dreams. The National Weather Service keeps track of Mother Nature's activity, but it does not have a crystal ball to predict it. It can warn us to prepare, and it can play Monday-morning quarterback to evaluate itself.

Some natural disasters have occurred on a grand, unimaginable scale. Because of media coverage, the world has been able to witness some crises before, during, and after they have taken place.

During Hurricane Katrina, observers wondered if they would have had the stamina, courage, and will to survive that some residents of New Orleans demonstrated by chopping holes in their roofs, climbing out, and exposing themselves to hurricane-force winds and rain, and waiting—not knowing if they would be spotted or rescued by an SAR (search and rescue) team or the volunteer, impromptu Cajun navy.

Not onlyAmericans but also people around the world shared the experience. We called it collective grief. The pain from that natural disaster rippled far beyond Louisiana. Everyone empathized, felt the pain, and went through the same steps of mourning as the individuals in New Orleans. Mutual mourning unites the world and has followed significant events such as wars, natural disasters like the tsunamis in Japan and Indonesia, school shootings, terrorist attacks, mass shootings, coronavirus pandemic, and deaths of public figures.

Our lives are touched and changed when we experience the suffering simultaneously. We are comforted with mutual humanitarian empathy.

***

We can grieve collectively. We have all grieved individually. I have been on both sides of grief and grieving. I have grieved, but I never imagined that I would be mourning my own loss of health due to a childhood illness. My symptoms of grief transitioned into the mourning process once I received a terminal diagnosis.

Of all the stages of grief I experienced, depression was the most difficult.

Five years ago, heart damage caused by rheumatic fever caught up with me. The beginning of the end was in Petra where a Bedouin chief came to my aid when I experienced a cardiac episode. Soon after my return home from that trip, I couldn't breathe. I was rushed to the emergency room where they wrapped me in copper blankets and prepared me to be airlifted to the heart hospital in Norfolk.

There, they told me that there was nothing that they could do for me. I signed the DNR (Do Not Resuscitate) papers, and they arranged for my final days to be spent in hospice where I was engaged in grief, grieving and healing with other residents.

Friends and relatives in various stages of the grief came or called to grieve and to say goodbye, I did not have the strength to comfort them in their grief, and their telling me that I would be in a better place was never a comfort to me.

What was a comfort was a diversion so I didn't have to think about dying, I understood how important my visit to the leprosy hospital had been to provide a respite from grieving.

I welcomed members of my chapel who brought me an angel holding the message "BELIEVE!" I did believe! I might have been the only one who believed I was not dying. One friend did bring me a lipstick. It was such a symbol of hope to me; it made me think that I might go outside again someday. Friends could anticipate my passing; but in the midst of my grieving, I could still hope for a miracle, and a miracle occurred. A brilliant cardiologist, Albert A. Burton, MD, had a plan. It was the first glimmer of hope.

He arranged surgery for me at a medical college in Richmond, where a surgeon from India replaced my mitral valve with a titanium valve in an experimental surgery. During his post-surgery visit, he could see that I could already breathe effortlessly and that my health had improved!

Since the surgery, I can now walk and talk simultaneously —a first in my life. In a quiet room, I can hear the mechanical valve; it is a comforting sound. Two years later I am ready for more adventures.

I am grateful for my experiences and my personal process through the stages of grief. Leaving the past behind and stepping into the future is a sign of healing readiness.

When we leave the past behind and step into the future, we have been given another opportunity to fulfill our purpose, whatever it is. My purpose might be to share my experiences through my writing —just in case a reader can glean some message to apply personally.

***

Because it is an emotion, there is no cure to eliminate the horrors that the terrorist called grief inflicts. Grief can never be eliminated because emotions cannot be extinguished. There is no cure for emotion. Emotions are to be expressed, not cured or suppressed.

It hurts more than anything to lose someone, and there is no correct way to express that emotion. It is subjective —what anyone feels is true; and the way feelings are expressed is the correct way, the right way, and the true way for that individual. Allowing one's authentic self to emerge by expressing feelings is a major step on the road to recovery.

There is no cure for grieving because grieving itself is an act of healing. Grief is not easy. Grieving is not easy. Life is not easy. Life is not fair.

Grief cannot be cured, but a mourner can be healed. There is no shortcut or hack for healing; advancing through the grieving process is a way to take action to heal. It is a difficult process, but it is the only way to cheat the terrorist grief and reclaim a semblance of the life that existed before the pain of grief pillaged it. If you are grieving, you are not alone.

The steps to take in grieving are difficult, and people who grieve often develop physical symptoms from the stress. Forewarned is forearmed.

Taking care of oneself is vital to a mourner's health. Preparations are basic, but sometimes must be forced. Remembering to take care of one's responsibilities (especially to other individuals or pets) might seem daunting. Eating, bathing, dressing, and taking care of necessities are all steps towards recovery.

There is no shame in asking for help from friends and supporters who want to help but not infringe on your privacy. Tell them what you want or need, dismiss well-meaning but unsolicited advice.

If you are supporting someone who is grieving, be kind and gentle. Be positive.

From my own experience as a griever and a potential bereaved, a person's presence (physically or virtually) is welcomed. Just listen, a griever needs to talk. Feel honored if someone opens up, but do not force anyone to talk. Offer to bring groceries or a treat. Be patient and compassionate. Don't expect anyone to be gleeful.

Many are going through stages of grieving. I have witnessed people around the world in various stages of the process. The most encouraging was a double amputee in a wheelchair on a pig farm in Vietnam. When I met him, I apologized for America and said I really didn't understand the Vietnam War. He called it "the *American* War." He told me that he did not hate me or any Americans. His was the most forgiving and sweetest heart.

He made it. He has gone through his grieving steps and made it to the final one: acceptance. He has earned the reward of stepping into the future.

Now more than ever, we should all be aware that people are fragile and carry burdens of physical and emotional hurt and pain. We need to show compassion and understanding as we meet and greet others gently. We can neutralize the terrorist grief with our love, hope, and compassion.

In Memory
of Anasofia

The Healing Journey
after Losing a Child

Anapaula Corral

*O*ur lives may be sometimes bittersweet, but they are also miraculous. Even if it's for a short period, every second you breathe counts. The same is true for our loved ones. Every moment shared with our loved ones is significant.

If we look—really look—what bits of holiness can we find today? I glance around me at this very moment, and I see the lovely branches of the palm trees outside my window. I see the photos of my family. I see my hands; I touch my body; I feel my warm breath as I inhale and exhale; I feel my heartbeat…

I may be sad when I miss my daughter, but today the gratitude for having her is greater than the sorrow. My heart is still capable of loving, forgiving, and coping.

Today, I see the cozy space that shelters me as I pen these thoughts. I feel protected, I feel at peace, and, somehow, I have managed to put back together my heart, which for many years was shattered and silent.

In the year 2006, my daughter passed away. The day she died was the saddest day in my life. I really don't know how I made it through that day. It was the worst, most sad day any human being could experience. There is no word that can describe the pain, the emptiness in my heart, and the sorrow.

Losing a child before their first birthday is an indescribable and heart-wrenching experience. It's more than the loss of a loved one; it's the shattering of dreams, hopes, and the future that parents envisioned for their child. The pain is profound, and the grief is overwhelming. In just one year, parents form a deep bond with their child; that time is filled with countless moments of joy, laughter, and love. When that journey is abruptly cut short, the emotional toll is immense. It's an enduring ache, a void that can never be fully filled.

For those who have experienced such a devastating loss, compassion and support are crucial as they navigate the complex emotional fallout and healing process. Grieving is a complicated and personal experience that varies from person to person. While it's not accurate to say that no one likes to grieve, many people may find the process challenging and uncomfortable.

Grieving involves confronting and processing intense emotions such as sadness, anger, and loss. Many people find it difficult to face these emotions and may try to avoid the pain associated with grieving. Grieving requires individuals to be vulnerable and open about their feelings. Some people may perceive vulnerability as a weakness or may fear being judged, either of which can lead to denying grief and avoiding the grieving process.

Social norms and expectations can influence how individuals express and cope with grief. Different cultures may have unique ways of dealing with grief. In some cultures, grieving openly is encouraged, while in others, it may be a more private and internal process. In those cultures or communities that discourage open displays of emotion, it may be challenging for individuals to grieve in a way that feels natural. This has been a major problem for many, and I do not agree with any of these.

Fear of the unknown amidst grieving can lead to an uncertain and unfamiliar journey. People may fear the unknown aspects of the grieving process, including how long it will last and what the outcome will be.

This fear may lead some individuals to resist or delay the grieving process.

In certain cultures or communities where there is a stigma associated with grief, individuals may fear judgment or criticism for expressing their grief openly, either of which can lead to the suppressing of their emotions.

Some individuals develop coping mechanisms, such as avoidance or distraction, to deal with difficult emotions. These coping strategies can hinder the natural grieving process, as individuals may not allow themselves the time and space to grieve.

The topic of losing a child is often considered taboo due to the intense emotional pain and societal discomfort surrounding it. Society tends to avoid discussing subjects that evoke deep grief, sadness, and vulnerability. Losing a child is a heartbreaking experience that challenges societal norms, and people may be hesitant to bring it up out of fear of causing additional pain or not knowing how to respond. Additionally, cultural and religious beliefs may contribute to the taboo nature of discussing child loss. Different cultures may have varying perspectives on grief, death, and appropriate ways to address such sensitive topics.

It's important to note that breaking the taboo around discussing child loss can be crucial for providing support and understanding to those who have experienced such a profound loss. Encouraging open conversations and fostering empathy can help create a more compassionate and supportive community for individuals dealing with grief. Everyone copes with grief differently, and there is no right or wrong way to grieve. Encouraging open conversations about grief, providing support, and fostering a compassionate environment can help individuals navigate the grieving process more effectively.

Death is often considered sad because it involves the permanent loss of someone or something we care about. It is a significant and inevitable part of the human experience, and the emotions associated with death, such as grief and sadness, are natural responses to the profound impact it has on individuals and communities. The sadness may stem from the sense of loss, the absence of the person or thing, and the realization that life is finite. People often mourn the memories, connections, and experiences that they shared with the deceased. Additionally, cultural and societal norms contribute to the perception of death as a somber and emotional event.

So, yes, losing any of your loved ones is sad, and the timing of that loss is uncertain. However, there are many things you can do to change your state of mind and slowly try to find emotional balance.

Stages that can help you put your heart back together after it has been shattered due to the loss of a child:

Aknowledging the Pain

Grieve is a verb, and if you ever experience losing a child—or if you know anyone who is going through this—you will find that each person's grief is unique, and the grieving process is nonlinear. You will be emotionally, physically, and psychologically impacted. Write a journal.

Finding the Power of Inner Work

Introspection and self-reflection. Counseling, sharing with similar groups, and keeping active.

Being Resilient and Recovering

Share uplifting stories while navigating grief. Highlight the common threads of strength, courage, and perseverance in these stories.

Using Support Systems

Talk about the significance of having a support system, including family, neighbors, friends, and professional help. Highlight the role of empathy and understanding in fostering healing.

Finding Meaning

Explore how individuals can find meaning in their grief, perhaps through advocacy, creative outlets, or community involvement. Discuss the concept of post-traumatic growth and how it can be a transformative force.

Embracing Joy

Share stories of individuals who have found moments of joy and happiness after their profound sorrow. Discuss the importance of allowing oneself to experience joy without guilt.

Knowing the Journey Is Ongoing

Summarize the transformative power of healing. Emphasize that the journey continues, and healing is an ongoing process.

***

I also have several thoughts that I would like to share. These are general notes I have written in all the years I have worked on putting my shattered heart back together. It is my hope they will inspire you to heal.

Evolving

Human life is a series of attachments, transitions, and losses. We explore; we connect; we love. We grow; we change; we lose.

Over and over on our journey through life, we experience hurt. We often equate the death of a loved one with the term "loss." But, really, it's just one kind of loss. Many other losses are deeply consequential as well, from health and financial problems to divorce, estranged relationships, abuse, betrayals, traumatic events, moves from beloved places, lost or broken dreams, and more. Even happy, appropriate transitions can be partly painful, such as leaving for college, getting married, and seeing children into adulthood.

All these significant losses can be deeply hurtful. When they arise, we naturally grieve inside. But most of us haven't learned that, just as with death, it's essential to mourn—or express our grief—over them. It is through mourning that we integrate all our losses along life's path. It is through mourning that we heal and learn to live well with ever-deeper joy and meaning.

Grieving and mourning our life losses take intention and commitment. The good news is that you can mourn while living a meaningful life.

Navigating the Duality of Life and Death

No matter how much we wish for a life of sunshine and smooth sailing, the world always finds a way of humbling us. We're young until we're not. We're healthy until we receive a devastating diagnosis. We're with those we love until they're taken from us. Forests burn while the birds sing. Life's beauty is inseparable from its fragility.

This "bothness"—the persistent, sometimes painful duality of life—is a cornerstone of emotional agility. You're experiencing bothness when a career change both thrills and terrifies you in equal measure. It's present when your child has disappointed you, and you love them all the same. Bothness exists in our capacity to welcome conflicting emotions—to feel joy at having known someone even as we grieve when they've passed on.

This bothness—the integration into your life of all emotions, even the challenging ones—is a litmus test of psychological health and well-being. It is the ability of an individual to recognize a difficult emotion or experience as being part of them without allowing it to define their identity or dictate their actions. Mixing or integration is when we refuse to classify our feelings as inherently good or bad, and instead accept them as part of the experience of being human.

The opposite of integration is segmentation or separation. Segmentation happens when we separate our lives into things we think about and things we do not think about, places we go and places we do not go, topics we discuss and those that are off-limits. It often rears its head during challenging times. If a couple ignores a source of conflict within their relationship, they drive a wedge between them, cordoning off that topic with a No Entry sign. When a leader perceives an employee feels an organizational change is negative, rather than a signal that the employee is invested in their job, it is an erosion of that employee's psychological safety in the workplace. But reliance on segmentation is unsustainable. It doesn't match our lived reality, in which life's darkest and most joyful moments, interwoven, create its beauty.

We see the rigidity of segmentation all around us, from our adherence to traditional professional hierarchies, to the way we talk to our children, to the harmful or divisive. We assume leaders have the answers, so we don't ask rookies for their perspectives. Instead of acknowledging that riding a bike without training wheels is both frightening and achievable, we tell our kids, "It's not that scary." And when a loved one tries to broach a topic that makes us anxious, we shut down instead of opening a dialogue and trying to achieve an understanding. But effective coping rarely involves turning away and shutting down. After all, how will we ever have truly meaningful conversations if we can't stand to face discomfort?

Bothness allows you to engage with people whose values depart from your own. It allows you to understand that a conversation with someone who thinks differently from you doesn't negate what you hold dear. Indeed, it is often the choice not to reach out and engage that is antithetical to your values. There is wisdom in bothness. We can move forward in hope and in fear, respecting the contradictions inside each one of us. Bothness gives us access to the full spectrum of life. Too often, we think that the world is a series of either/or decisions. Be bold. Choose both.

Living in the Present Moment
Living in the moment and cherishing time with loved ones is a crucial aspect of leading a fulfilling and meaningful

life. Here are some ways to describe the importance of this:

- Limited Time Frame: Life is finite, and time is a limited resource. Embracing the present allows us to fully experience and appreciate the moments we have with our loved ones. Recognizing the transient nature of time encourages us to make the most of each moment.

- Strong Connections: Living in the moment fosters deeper connections with those we care about. When we are fully present, we engage more authentically with others, which strengthens our relationships. These shared experiences create lasting memories that contribute to the forming of strong bonds.

- Mindfulness and Well-Being: Being present in the moment involves practicing mindfulness, which has been linked to improved mental and emotional well-being. It reduces stress, anxiety, and worry about the future or past. Cherishing time with loved ones in the present contributes to a more positive and peaceful state of mind.

- Absence of Regrets: Regret often stems from missed opportunities or neglecting the present. By cherishing moments with loved ones as they happen, we minimize the likelihood of regret later in life. It allows us to look back without wishing we had been more present in certain situations.

- Positive Atmosphere: Living in the moment contributes to a positive atmosphere in our relationships. It allows us to appreciate the small joys, express gratitude, and focus on the positives, which creates an uplifting environment for ourselves and our loved ones.

- Quality Over Quantity: It's not just about the amount of time spent with loved ones, but the quality of that time. Being present ensures that the time we share is meaningful and enjoyable, which leads to more enriching experiences.

- Balance in Priorities: In the hustle and bustle of life, it's easy to get caught up in various responsibilities. Living in the moment helps us strike a balance between work, personal pursuits, and time with loved ones. It reminds us of the importance of prioritizing relationships.

In summary, living in the moment and cherishing time with loved ones is a conscious choice that adds depth, joy, and fulfillment to our lives. It's about savoring the present, building lasting connections, and embracing the beauty of shared experiences.

Leaving a Family Legacy

The death of a child can drastically change the family legacy; the profound impact of losing a child has the potential to reshape the narrative and trajectory of the family's legacy. Traditionally, a family legacy might be seen as a continuation, through generations, of the values, traditions, and accomplishments that have been passed down. However, the death of a child introduces a tragic and unexpected element that can alter this narrative.

The child's legacy will be different if we choose to see it can also contribute to society and create a legacy of its own amidst the grief and the pain. Despite the heartbreak and pain, there is an opportunity to reinterpret the legacy left by the child. Instead of focusing solely on the loss, one can choose to recognize the potential for the child's impact on society and the positive legacy that can emerge from their memory.

- Shift in Perspective: A shift in perspective from viewing the child's legacy solely through the lens of loss and grief, to considering the positive contributions and impact the child had during their time.

- Contribution to Society: Even in the face of tragedy, the child's legacy can extend beyond the family unit. This could involve acknowledging the positive qualities, values, or actions of the child that may have had a broader impact on the community or society.

- Legacy of Positivity amidst Grief: Despite the grief and pain associated with the loss, there is an invitation to create a legacy that encompasses positivity and meaningful contributions. This could involve memorializing the child through acts of kindness, charity, or initiatives that honor their memory.

- Recognition of Individuality: Each person, including a child, has a unique impact on the world. By recognizing and celebrating the individuality of the child, one can create a legacy that reflects their personality, interests, and the positive aspects of their presence.

- Inspiration for Others: The acknowledgment of a child's potential contribution to society, even in a short life, can serve as inspiration for others. It may motivate individuals to make a positive impact and cherish the moments they have with their loved ones.

- Narrative of Hope: Amidst the grief, there is an opportunity to shape a narrative of hope, resilience, and positive change. It encourages the family to focus on the enduring impact the child and the potential for that impact to continue in meaningful ways.

- Legacy of Resilience: Families may find strength in creating a legacy of resilience. This could involve supporting each other, engaging in charitable activities in memory of the child, or participating in support groups to help others going through similar experiences.

- Remembrance and Honor: Families may choose to remember and honor the child in various ways, such as creating a memorial, establishing a scholarship fund, or participating in events that commemorate the child's life. These acts contribute to a positive legacy in the face of tragedy.

- Impact on Future Relationships: The loss of a child can impact how family members approach future relationships and life decisions. It may influence perspectives on parenting, priorities, and the importance of cherishing moments with loved ones.

The power of choosing to see the child's legacy, not just in terms of loss, but as an opportunity to contribute positively to society. It encourages a perspective that acknowledges the child's unique legacy and the potential for creating a lasting impact that goes beyond the immediate grief and pain.

***

In the face of profound loss, we embark on a journey of healing, a path marked by the echoes of cherished memories. While the pain of losing a family member may never fully subside, our ability to endure and find solace reveals the strength within us. Just as wounds may fade, the love and shared moments linger, guiding us towards a space where healing coexists with the enduring spirit of those we hold dear. In this tapestry of loss and healing, we discover the resilience to navigate life's complexities, knowing that the indomitable bond of love transcends the boundaries of time and space.

My deep wish for you is that you can pick up the pieces of your shattered heart and start your healing journey. You are not alone.

In Memory of
Arthur Frank King

My Great-Uncle Art

This Was His Life

Angela Gilson

*A*rthur Frank King was born on May 4, 1936, to Waldo T. King and Helen E. King in Vaugh, near Sedro-Woolley, in the state of Washington. Art always had a smile on his face and was ambitious. During high school, he bought, refurbished, and resold seventeen old cars, worked for the *Olympia Daily News*, managed a local drugstore, and still made time for varsity cheerleading. He graduated with honors from Olympia High in 1954.

That same year, he joined the United States Air Force, where he trained as an aircraft mechanic. Shortly after basic training, he was stationed at Blytheville Air Force Base in Arkansas, where he met Kathleen Kent (my great-aunt), the love of his life, in February 1956.

At that time, she worked in a drive-in called Kream Kastle. When she first saw him, she knew in her heart she was going to marry him. When she took his order, he wanted to play a prank on her, so he ordered a pine float (water with a toothpick in it). She knew what it was, so she brought it to him.

He and his buddies in the car laughed because she got the joke. He came back every night for two weeks, looking for her to ask her out on a date and to take her home at the end of her shift.

When she said yes to a date, she wanted a girl from work to go with them. When they went on dates, it had to be after her night shift at work, so they went to the movies and dinner together.

Arthur and Kathleen married June 9, 1956, had their first son, Steven, born December 24, 1960, at Ladd Air Force Base, where Arthur was stationed. He was soon transferred to an army base, Fort Wainwright, in Alaska. There, they had their second, Jerry, on September 9, 1962. They spent the next sixty-three years together, traveling the world and sharing addresses from Alaska to Florida, Montana to Texas, and overseas from Newfoundland, Holland, and Thailand.

Their favorite place was Alaska. They both loved living there and regularly fishing and camping. Art was a decorated Vietnam War veteran who was awarded numerous medals and commendations throughout his twenty-three years of service. He served as a senior crew chief on multiple aircrafts and weapon systems, including the B-26, B-52, B-57, KC-135, F-89, T-33, F-100, F-101, F-104, F-4, A-37, AU-23, AU-24, C-5, C-17, and a few experimental ones.

While serving, Uncle Art received a bachelor's degree from Chicago University and later a master's degree from Southwest Texas State. As a hobby, he worked on many civilian aircraft for local aeronautics clubs. He eventually earned his private pilot's license and built and owned his own planes.

He retired from the United States Air Force in 1977. Yet, the Air Force never really left him. After a few aircraft-mechanic teaching jobs, he rejoined the Air Force as a civil servant at Kelly Air Force Base. He managed the military's largest airplane of the time, the C-5 Galaxy.

Uncle Art decided to retire for the second time in 1998. They bought land in Texas, and he built his own home from the ground up; family members helped, including my dad. Uncle Art had his own boat, and he went fishing on the canyon lake where he lived. He took his kids, beautiful granddaughter, nieces, and nephews all over the countryside, including Washington, California, and New

Mexico. He loved taking them to the ocean. His favorite hobbies were working on his planes, old cars, hunting, and fishing.

My Uncle Art, he wasn't just an uncle; he was a grandpa to me. I will always remember him as a funny, kind, and caring man who walked my grandma down the aisle and gave her away to my grandfather. He was like a father figure to my aunt Louise's kids who had lost their father. He stepped up, was there for them, and helped when they needed him.

I will always remember the trip we took to the jellybean factory, the funny poses we made at the beach, the sand castles we built, the ocean as we walked together in the water, and the pancakes at dinnertime when he and my grandma visited us. I remember his voice and will carry his warm hugs with me for the rest of my life.

I remember the time when Uncle Art and Aunt Kathy came to our home in California from Texas; Uncle Art and my dad put down wood floors and kitchen tiles in our home. They also built my mom an entertainment center. I learned a lot from watching him and my dad work together. Uncle Art also taught me about his RV and how it worked.

When we were at the dinner table, and I was really hungry and couldn't wait to eat, he noticed. So he took a couple of bites, and so did I. Then he went, "Shh," with a smile on his face. After that, everyone at the table said grace before the meal. I loved when Uncle Art said the grace.

Uncle Art was always devoted to his family, friends, and faith. He was a charter member of Grace Bible Church, where he participated in many leadership roles, deacon council, small groups, and men's group. He engaged in the community, the local VFW, and participated in a variety of service groups. His missionary spirit led him to support Gideons International and personally visit with the children of VivaKids.

Last time I saw Uncle Art was after work when they visited us. I had to get my last picture with him because, not long after that, a few months later, he passed away. We all knew he was sick in the beginning, so I said my goodbyes over the phone while my dad visited him. I told him he was like a grandpa to me. He choked up and almost started crying.

That day, he passed away. I was in college, and my dad texted me. My dad barely texts or calls, so at that moment, I knew Uncle Art had died. I cried silently in my dorm room. My boyfriend at the time had to pick me up off the floor. He asked what happened. I told him my Uncle Art had passed. He asked if my parents had told me, but I said no. I just knew he had passed. It breaks my heart till this day that I couldn't be there with him in person to give him one last hug.

That night, I remember as if it were yesterday. I woke from a nightmare at 4:30 a.m. I usually go for walks when I'm upset. Little did I know I wanted to go home, so I walked home that night, which turned out to be around a three-hour walk.

I didn't get home until around seven, right at sunrise. I didn't have a key; I had left it in my dorm. So I rang the doorbell. My parents were surprised that I was there at the front door. I went into my room, and they both followed me. My parents had sad faces. My dad sat next to me on my bed, and my mom was on the brink of tears.

They told me Uncle Art had passed away. I told them I already knew. They looked surprised and asked how I knew. I told my dad he never texts me, so that's how I knew. My dad, who doesn't show emotions, told me it was okay to cry because he wasn't just an uncle to us; he was a dad and a grandpa. My parents didn't want to tell me until class was over, but I already knew he had passed without them even telling me.

I remember, before school started, I got from Aunt Kathy a beautiful sea-turtle necklace, which I still have. Whenever I miss Uncle Art, I grab the sea turtle in my hands and remember him and his warm hug. I think just having that beautiful necklace helps me through it. I also pray to him and for his soul to find peace because he is no longer in pain.

At age eighty-three, Uncle Art passed away peacefully in his sleep on November 4, 2019, in Canyon Lake, Texas, from diabetes, which is what he suffered from for a long time. He is survived by his wife, Kathleen King; son, Jerry King, and wife, Beverly Luce; granddaughter, Caitlin King; brother, Alan King; sister, Joanne, and husband, Bill Brotten; and by a bounty of other family, in-laws, nieces, and nephews. He was preceded in death by his oldest son, Steven King, and brother, Douglas King. Uncle Art was buried on Friday, November 15, at Fort Sam Houston National Cemetery.

While I was grieving the loss of my uncle, I wanted to be alone most of the time. When I was alone, I coped by listening to music. That's how I express my emotions and let them out.

My Uncle Art will live within us. What my dad learned from his uncle, he is teaching me. We will always have the memories of dinners and places we visited. At the time of his death, I was already seeing a counselor, so we both talked about that night; the counselor said that I had a manic episode.

As a family, we talk about the loss of Uncle Art, but my dad keeps telling me that he was sick for a long time. But he had an amazing, long life and was surround by loved ones when he passed.

It Pays to Just Listen

Conrad M. Gonzales

*A*fter retiring from the San Antonio Fire Department in 1998 as a firefighter and paramedic, I often wondered if there would ever be another moment that I needed to put my paramedic skills to use. Would it be saving someone from choking? Applying a tourniquet? Saving a drowning victim? Or just saving a life by telling someone to make sure they buckle up? I thought to myself, *I hope not.*

Well, three weeks prior to writing this piece, I did, in fact, perform the abdominal thrusts on my mom as she started to choke while we were having lunch! That's the sixth time I had to save the life of a family member! My daughter, three times; my sister, twice; and now my mom. I pray that I don't have to do this again. But what can I say? I'm ready if I have to.

Now, let's rewind back to the year 2005. I was working as a parent educator for males and as a case manager for a nonprofit agency that catered to families here in San Antonio. Yes, a fatherhood program teaching fathers of all ages how to be better dads. This, of course, included grandfathers as well. This position had me traveling anywhere that provided parenting instructions to fathers young and old.

One day, while I was sitting in my office, my phone rang, and I thought it was someone who needed parenting classes. I answered the phone and introduced myself. After a few moments of silence, I introduced myself again and asked who was on the other end of the line.

It was a male who whispered that he wanted to kill himself. I sat there stunned. I was speechless. He continued to tell me that he no longer wanted to live because his wife had left him; she took the kids with her. I asked him for his name. Robert was what he told me. I proceeded to first thank him for calling me, and then I told him that I wanted to do whatever I could to help him. Silence followed. I waited for him to respond. He then continued telling me that he was at a point where he didn't care at all, and he wanted to end his life.

I had to think fast. This actually brought back memories of another gentleman I came across while I was working in EMS as a paramedic. He had a knife to his throat and was going through the same thing. Now, that's another story.

I asked Robert if he had a plan, and he said he did. He wanted to hang himself. By the tone of his voice, I knew he was serious. I immediately asked him where he was. He responded that he was at home, but he didn't want anyone to come over, and he didn't want the police or EMS to show up. He threatened that if he heard the sirens, he was close enough to just walk over to his garage and do it before the emergency vehicles arrived.

With a sigh of relief, I knew I had some time to try to talk him out of it. I told him that we all go through all kinds of troubles in our lives; he was not the only one. I mentioned to him that I, too, was blindsided and shocked when I was given divorce papers and thought of how my young children would react and suffer as well. I then paused so he could continue talking to me.

Robert stated that he worked his butt off to provide food, shelter, and clothing for his children; he also tended to his wife's needs, from clothing to a nice car. He worked two, and sometimes three, jobs. He kept repeating that he did not deserve going through this torture and that he couldn't take it anymore.

We were on the phone for over twenty minutes when I offered to drive over to his house so we could sit down and talk. He refused my offer. He said there wasn't anything I could do for him. I asked him to just let me come over there, and I promised him that I would not call the police or EMS. He finally agreed. He gave me his street address, and as I told him thank you, I mentioned that I knew exactly where the street was because I used to work at the fire station a few miles north of where he lived.

I asked him, before hanging up, if he had any weapons, such as a gun or knife, on him or nearby. He said he did not. I told him that I trusted him, and I didn't want him to hurt me or try to kill me because I had children and people who cared about me. And if he tried to do something, I would die fighting him. He reassured me that he did not have any weapons at all. I informed him that I would be there in twenty minutes and asked him to please trust me. He responded by telling me that he trusted me and would wait. I got in my car and was on the highway in less than three minutes.

On my way to Robert's house, I was thinking about that call I went on as a paramedic, the one with the gentleman who was holding a knife to his own throat.

I asked myself, *Should I be doing this? Am I risking my life for someone I don't even know? Should I call the police or EMS?* I thought that it was actually my job back then, but here, now, was a human being who needed some help.

To this day, I have no idea how and why he called me at the office. Had I met him before? Had our paths crossed at some time? Had he attended any of my classes? At this point, it didn't matter. He needed someone to talk to. I needed to listen, and we needed to trust each other.

As I turned onto his street, I remember Robert's description of the house. It was an older one-story home with a white picket fence around the yard and red rose-bushes in front of the house. With the yard beautifully manicured, it was easy to spot. I stopped the car, stepped out, and started to cross the street and head toward the porch. I was looking around to see if there was a gun or rifle poking out a window or door. This, I learned from friends who were police officers. They would tell me to be observant "because you never know." So I looked to see if doors were made out of wood or steel, and I checked for alternative means of escape. Unfortunately, the only exit point I saw, should I need one, was the front door.

I knocked on the door. There was no answer. I knocked again and quietly yelled that it was Conrad. Then I heard footsteps on what sounded like a wooden floor. It sounded as if he was wearing boots. He opened the door slowly as he peeked around it; I could only see half of his face. He asked if there was anyone else with me. I assured him, just as I told him, that no one came with me. He opened the door and let me in. Yep, he was wearing boots, and I was correct—wooden floors.

I thanked him for letting me in as we walked slowly into the living room. I could see why he was devastated. The house was empty except for the dining room table and four chairs. He was right. She took everything in the house, even the refrigerator.

As we sat down at the table, Robert began to cry as he continued telling me how "messed up" it was for his wife to leave him without even a single notion or warning that she was tired of being his wife and that she wanted out of the relationship. There was a note on the dining room table. He grabbed it and showed it to me. He told me to read it.

In the note, Robert's wife described how the last few years were intolerable, and she just didn't love him anymore. "You're never home," the note read. He described how his wife had always wanted to "keep up with the neighbors" who bought better homes, cars, and went on vacations. Robert then explained that his plan was to work two, maybe three, jobs to please her and try to live the same lifestyle as the neighbors.

I asked Robert how long they'd been married.

"We've been married for nine years. Next week would have been ten."

I applauded him for doing what he could to make his wife happy, but told him, sometimes, that doesn't help. Working your butt off can lead to distress and increase the likelihood of heart disease, high blood pressure, and other ailments. He mentioned that he had high blood pressure, and his family had a history of diabetes. He'd been to the doctor a few weeks earlier and was told that he needed to be compliant in taking his medication as prescribed. I asked him if he was, and he responded by telling me that he "was and then wasn't."

I told him that he really needed to take care of himself if he wanted to see his kids. That struck a nerve. He started crying again and stated that she wasn't going to let him see the kids. I reassured him that he would see his kids again, but that it would take time, patience, perseverance, and a lot of prayers. I told him that, once, I didn't get to see my son for a year, and that hurt. But the courts finally decided in my favor and gave me joint custody, which was out of the norm back in those days.

As Robert finally calmed down, I came to the decision that I had to talk to him about his plan to kill himself. He said he was going to hang himself in the garage, where no one would find him. I asked him where he worked. He refused to say. I explained to him that, no matter where he worked, someone would miss him, and they'd come over to his house and conduct a welfare check. I continued to tell him that he didn't want to put any of his friends, coworkers, or family members through the trauma of finding him hanging in the garage. I'd seen it several times in my career as a paramedic in EMS.

I proceeded with our conversation by telling him to take me to the garage. We slowly stood up and moved toward the back door, which led to his back porch. As we walked, I placed my hand on his shoulder. He opened the back door, and as we stepped off the back porch, I saw that we were headed to the side door of his garage. He opened that door and led me in.

The garage was poorly lit. I asked Robert if there was a light and, if so, to turn it on so I could see. As the light came on, I looked up and saw it—the rope. It was hanging from the rafter. The rope had a noose at the end, and below the noose was a barstool. I stood still. He was serious.

I looked at Robert and asked if he had a box cutter. He walked over to his workshop area and reached for a box cutter on the workbench. As he walked back toward me, I stopped him and told him to grab his ladder. He asked why. I looked him in the eye and told him that if he had the guts to climb it to set the noose, he should have the guts to cut it down. He stared at me for a moment before walking over and grabbing the ladder.

Robert moved the barstool and placed the ladder under the noose. As he started to climb up, I grabbed hold of the ladder. He looked down and seemed to wonder why I was grabbing the ladder.

I told him, "I don't want you to fall. It's called 'footing the ladder.' It's a firefighter thing."

He turned back around and continued to climb. I was actually grabbing the ladder in the event he decided to place the noose around his neck and kick the ladder away.

Robert reached up, grabbed the noose, and cut the rope. He handed the noose to me, and I then tossed it to the garage floor. He climbed down and stepped off the ladder. I grabbed a plastic bag that was on the floor and placed inside it the noose along with the rest of the rope. In the open bag, I noticed a receipt and took it out. Looking at it, I noticed it had that day's date. He'd bought the rope and the barstool two hours before he called me.

I looked at Robert, thanked him, and told him, "You have a life to live...now, you have a life to give. Robert, today you are making a difference in your life and the lives of your children. With time and prayers, you'll heal. It may take a while, and I can't promise you how long, but you'll slowly heal. I want you to look forward to talking to and seeing your kids. With time, patience, and prayer, you'll feel better."

He looked at me and said, "Thank you."

I replied, "No, thank you for calling me and trusting me to be here with you."

We both turned around and stepped out of the garage. As I was walking behind him, I turned around to close the garage door. As I was doing that, I looked up to see where the rope had hung from the rafter. I took a deep breath and thought, *Thank you, Lord.*

I followed Robert and walked into the house. I had the bag in my hand. We walked to the dining room table and sat down again. As we did, the doorbell rang. I asked him if he was expecting anyone or if he had called anyone else.

He said no. He then asked me if I had called anyone. I reminded him that I promised not to call anyone or have anyone follow me. He got up, walked to the door, and stopped before opening it. He yelled to see who it was.

It was his sister. She had stopped by to check on him, as she had tried calling him earlier in the day. She was on her way home from work and had stopped to see how he was doing. She knew that he'd been having problems at home.

As she stepped in, she saw me sitting at the table. I stood up and introduced myself. Robert then told her that I was a friend who was visiting. It felt good that Robert now considered me a friend. Robert told her that I had come by, as he needed someone to talk to about his troubles.

Robert's sister looked around and noticed that all the furniture was gone. She seemed to be getting ready to ask Robert what happened, but he stopped her and said that everything was all right and that his wife had moved out. He then continued to tell her that he was fine and "my" friend Conrad was there to help. She turned and looked at me to thank me. She told me that she'd been trying to get someone to speak to Robert, but to no avail. I told her that things happen for a reason and that I was glad to be there for him. As she sat down at the table, I felt that it was time to leave Robert and his sister so they could talk.

Robert actually looked at me and said, "Thank you, Conrad. I got this."

I returned his gaze and said, "I know you do." I proceeded to the door; Robert walked with me and opened the door for me.

His sister then asked me as she looked down at the floor, "Sir, is this your bag?"

I told her, "Yes, thank you! I almost forgot it."

Little did she know what was in the bag and what had happened minutes before she arrived. She was reaching down for it when I told her not to worry; I would get it.

I picked the bag up, turned around, told Robert to call me anytime, and reminded him that he had my number. Then, we gave each other a big hug as he whispered, "Thank you, sir. You saved my life."

I responded, "We both did," as I stepped out the door and looked back at Robert as he closed the door. We gave each other a thumbs-up.

I walked to my car, opened the trunk, put the bag inside, and closed the trunk. I walked around and opened the car door, got in, started the car, and put on my seat belt. I turned to the left and looked over at Robert's house. It was dusk. Through the curtains, I could see the lights on in the dining room where Robert and I had sat. Now, there were two shadows, Robert and his sister. I took a deep breath, put my car in gear, and drove off.

As I was pulling out of the neighborhood, I had this feeling of relief, happiness, and exhaustion…emotional exhaustion. I felt drained as if I'd just gotten off work after a twenty-four-hour shift in EMS. I felt as though I were a tire with a slow leak, its pressure dropping so low the tire would soon be flat.

I called my supervisor at work. Something I hated doing while driving. I told her I would not be returning to work, as it was close to five o'clock. She asked me if I was all right. I told her I was just a little tired and going home to rest a bit and would see her the next day. She inquired about my whereabouts since I left without notifying her. I apologized and told her I had an emergency to tend to. I assured her everything was okay.

While driving, I was lost in my thoughts and thinking about Robert. Before I knew it, I was pulling into my driveway. I pulled up to my garage and stopped right in front of it. I reached for the remote to open the garage door but halted. I quickly remembered that my garage had exposed rafters. At that moment, I didn't really want to be reminded of what transpired at Robert's house.

I parked in the driveway, turned the car off, and stepped out of it. I then opened the trunk and took the bag out. I walked over to the garbage can, lifted the lid, and threw the bag into the garbage can. As the bag dropped in, I looked at it and said a quick prayer, "Thank you, Lord, for being there for me and for Robert." I then closed the lid and walked inside the house.

As I walked through my kitchen, I thought about Robert and how he must have felt as he walked into an empty house and found his wife and kids gone. I know it had to have been tough on him. He must have felt devastated and robbed of his life without his wife and children.

Emotionally drained, I walked into my bedroom and sat on the bed. I was grateful that I had a bed on which to sleep. I thought about Robert not having a bed, so I called him. The phone rang, and he answered. I asked him if he was okay, and he said he was fine and staying the night at his sister's house. I was relieved and assured him that I would be available if he needed anything.

He said, "Thanks, Conrad. I'm good now."

We hung up. I took off my shoes and shirt and laid my head on the pillow. I looked up at a picture of Jesus Christ, which was hanging on the wall. "I am with you every day," the caption read.

"Yes, He is. He was today."

Lying there, I remembered an important thing from my days in EMS. Whenever you come across a patient who is thinking about taking their own life, you have to be patient. Developing trust between you, as a paramedic, and your patient is tantamount to creating a positive outcome. Practicing patience, remaining calm, and, most important, listening play major roles in the end result.

Fast-forward to the year 2023—I spoke to Robert's sister and asked how he was doing. She said he was doing fine. He actually reunited with his wife not long after the incident; they have been together now for almost twenty years. She said they still have their ups and downs but have vowed to stay together. I told her to tell Robert hello for me and that I think about him and his family. For this piece, his sister said he declined to provide a photo of himself, as he wishes to remain anonymous. I told her that I understood, and we left it at that. I'm glad he's still with us.

One of many important characteristics of a first responder is the ability to listen. That day, Robert reached out, as he needed someone to talk to and someone to listen. I just happened to answer the phone when he called; ironically, the administrative assistant was on her break, and I just happened to answer the phone for her. It wasn't a coincidence; it was a "God-incidence."

One trait that my parents ingrained in me was the ability to let others talk and to lend an ear. I learned that characteristic at a very young age and carried it into my profession as a firefighter and paramedic. Witnessing countless injuries and deaths allowed me to learn and listen to those who were suffering from injuries or who had lost their loved ones. There were many times as a paramedic that I'd place my hand on someone's shoulder and quietly tell them, "I'm sorry for your loss. I'm here for you." They talked, grieved, and cried. And I listened.

Anger, denial, bargaining—these are some of the responses I witnessed when a spouse, child, brother, sister, mother, or father died. We were usually the first on the scene. This is why we're called first responders. We're the first to respond to those in need of assistance during a life-threatening crisis. That is our job. That is what I teach future EMTs and paramedics—how to respond in a crisis.

So how do we respond in a crisis? We respond to distress with eustress. Extreme anxiety, pain, and sorrow describe distress. Positivity and the ability to respond and cope in a positive and beneficial manner describe eustress. We must focus on reacting with eustress, as this will enhance the likelihood of a better outcome. Easier said than done, I've been told. Yes, but it *can* be done. All we have to do is reach out to someone and...listen.

In November of 2014, I wrote the following poem during a difficult time in my life as I was thinking that there IS light in the darkness. Hence the title, "The Lighter Side of Darkness." It is about finding positivity when grief and turmoil abound. I hope this poem keeps you healthy, safe, and sound.

"The Lighter Side of Darkness"

There are times in life when we suffer pain and sorrow,
and there seems as if there will be no tomorrow.
Pain is inflicted on our hearts and on our minds,
and solutions to despair may be impossible to seek or find.

There are times in life when tears will flow,
and when they stop, no one really knows.
Life will seem to be shadowed and obscured,
and in vain, we search for reasons and a cure.

There are times in life when darkness seems to take over,
and no one seems to be there to lean on or cry on their shoulder.
We never know when our time shall arrive,
so we must take charge of our feelings and our lives.

Darkness is a shadow cast upon our light.
What can we do to make things right?
Darkness is temporary only if we want it to be.
So we must make a change to live forever happily.

We must move from the shadow of darkness and seek the light.
We seek in ourselves peace and the God of Might.
The Lord allows us to see darkness to learn about love,
And pain is an ingredient of strength from above.

So love to be free and be free to love,
as we feel the breeze cast from a flying white dove.
The key to life after suffering and pain
is to heal through love and be happy again.

Let darkness be gone and be shed aside.
Let light shine upon us and be rid of our strife.
We move forward and ahead with love and happiness,
And we must always look at the
"Lighter Side of Darkness."

If you or anyone you know is contemplating suicide, having suicidal thoughts, or actively thinking about committing suicide, you can call the Suicide and Crisis Lifeline (formerly National Suicide Prevention Lifeline) at: 1-800-273-8255, dial 988, or text 741741l. Trained crisis counselors are available 24/7.

Where there is hope…there is help.

*In Memory
of "Sticks"*

Friendship and Grief

Dave Grunenwald

$\mathcal{A}$s I prepared to write, I asked my pastor, "Does humor play a role when grieving—for example, pulling a prank on a dying friend? What I am about to tell you occurred, but I am wondering if it is okay to write about it?"

He answered, "Grief and humor often go together. The word *funeral* starts with the word *fun*."

Sometimes, laughter is the best medicine. This is a story that combines grief and humor.

What is grief? Webster defines it as "deep sorrow, especially caused by someone's death." At one time or another, grief affects us all. How we choose to deal with grief is a very personal matter.

Recently, a friend told me shortly after losing his wife, "In the end, each of us deals with our own grief privately." We all respond differently—discussing the loss with others, becoming more active, taking up a hobby, joining a support group, and/or volunteering for a worthy cause, among other responses. I believe the key to grieving is staying connected to friends and family.

So, naturally, as I look back twenty years, toilet papering a good friend's Las Vegas home shortly before his death was more than appropriate.

It Starts with Friendship

I was blessed with a wonderful family. As one of eight kids, my immediate family now includes two daughters, two grandsons, and more than fifty nieces, nephews, great-nieces, and great-nephews.

I was equally blessed with a large group of friends, especially the ones mentioned in this story. They include Sticks, owing to his skill as a drummer (his strong hands also made him unbeatable at foosball); the Hunk, owing to his outstanding looks of which we were all jealous; the Voice, owing to his a cappella talents in high school and beyond (though not so much now); the Stud, owing to his being the best athlete among us; and the Kid, owing to his youthful appearance (he looks at seventy like his high school graduation picture). These were my best friends.

Growing up in Youngstown, Ohio, we went to three different high schools and graduated circa 1970. We knew each other's families well, including moms, dads, brothers, sisters, and often aunts, uncles, and grandparents. Later in life, we came to know each other's spouses and children. We remain great friends today, as do many of our children. Baptisms, graduations, weddings, and family reunions among us were the norm. These men were to become lifelong friends, the kind you treasure.

When we were kids, we knew most of our neighbors for blocks in all directions and had things in common, such as the schools we attended and parks where we played. I came to know the Kid in first grade. He, along with the Voice and the Hunk, became neighbors in high school when we moved. I eventually met Sticks and the Stud when we played softball together.

Leaving the house in the morning and returning for dinner was not unusual; our parents never really knew where we spent the day, though they had some idea, such as the local ball field or a friend's house. I was often at one friends' house one day, another the next, and so on and so on. Neighbors looked out for each other, including everyone's kids. Parents took it for granted, with good reason, we were safe.

Often, parents were not even home. Many worked. My mom was a good example. She raised eight kids and often worked or slept during the day, after the midnight shift as a nurse, so watching us during the day was unusual.

I have heard a few comedians over the years comment on kids being gone all day, our parents surprised if we came home before dinner. See some of Lewis Black's material. Seems like a foreign concept these days.

Friendship and Pranks

We were great pranksters too, especially during the high school and college years. Pranks were a way of showing our love for one another; they strengthened our friendships. Ours were basic pranks. Hiding things. Pretending to steal or misplace something. Making fake phone calls. Switching drinks in a bar. Nothing very sophisticated but great fun. A few were elaborate.

Today, pulling pranks and posting to social media for clicks, likes, and views is not the same. Not even close.

No doubt owing to our jealousy towards his good looks, the Hunk was often the target, though all of us were from time to time. Make no mistake, we loved the Hunk—we always will—as he is one of us.

After high school, the Hunk worked in the kitchen at a local hospital. One night, after he went to bed early at a sleepover, needing to rise early for work, we turned all the clocks in the house ahead to wake him early. We knew victory was at hand when we managed to turn ahead the time on the wristwatch he was wearing as he slept.

After rising and singing in the shower (he nearly woke my mother), he ate his usual breakfast of Diet Coke and Cocoa Puffs. Soon, the Voice drove him to work the long way about 5:00 a.m.—giving the rest of us time to arrive before him—instead of what he thought was 7:00 a.m., his usual start time. As they pulled up to the hospital entrance, we were waiting to let him know it was only 5:00 a.m. He was surprised, to say the least. Profanity may have been involved. The funny thing is he was written up at work for clocking in early.

Then, there was the time the Kid's sister rolled up the Hunk's dress shirt, ran it under the faucet, and placed it in the freezer. When he asked if anyone had seen his shirt, she replied, "Check the freezer." Upon its discovery, the look on his face and reaction were priceless.

There were dozens more like that. Pranks do have their poignant moments though.

Once Sticks and the Stud rearranged the furniture in my house. We lived on the second floor of a duplex with a common basement two floors below. It would have been funny, except it scared my younger sister when she returned from the basement after doing laundry. She was upset; so much so, she called Mom, who came home from work.

Returning shortly thereafter to witness my mother and sister sitting on the *living room couch in the dining room*, I asked, "Why is the couch in here?"

Mom simply said, "Your friends are at it again."

Of course, my mother believed it was the Hunk's doing, but told him she forgave him, knowing he was often the target of our pranks. For years, he reminded Mom he had not rearranged the furniture, but she took her belief to the grave.

I did not have the heart to tell her he was not the culprit. Sticks and the Stud had gotten off the hook.

About a year or so later, looking around the living room, for the first time I realized they had also rearranged the pictures on the walls; they were still hanging in the wrong places.

Loss of a Good Friend

Many of us knew grief at an early age from losing a family member—in my case, my father when I was five and my sister seven. Loss of a family member can be a devastating event in one's life. As you grow, you come to realize that death is a part of life as you learn to accept and live with it. Such acceptance makes you stronger.

Remember, though, when we were young, we thought sixty was old!

Later in life, I lost my beloved spouse of forty years and several siblings. My friends have had similar experiences. Death of a family member saddens you, often leaving a scar that lasts a lifetime. You come to expect the eventual loss of parents and grandparents, and other family members as well, though it is always difficult to deal with.

Losing a lifelong friend in the prime of his life is different than losing a family member. Not more painful or sadder. Different.

By the time you reach your fifties, and have a spouse and kids, and a house and mortgage, it is different. You settle into midlife, raise children, see them leave the roost or head off to college, as you and your spouse become empty nesters, plan to travel, and enjoy life as you slow down.

Then, one day, one of these dear friends gets sick.

We learned Sticks had cancer when departing for a golf trip; at the last minute, we found out he would not be joining us as usual. Our first reaction: Cancer? How can that be? He is so young. Why? We all had so many questions. To say the least, our mood on the trip was subdued.

Of course, we realized we had the easy part. We were never fully able to understand what he, his wife, and their two children must have been going though.

Sticks was in the prime of his life and looking to the future. After moving to Las Vegas in the '80s, he started and grew a successful business, had a wonderful wife and children, owned a beautiful home, and now had the best years of his life ahead.

Sticks was a jokester with an unforgettable laugh. He was typical of the others mentioned herein—smart, funny, deep sense of humor. The kind of friend who would do anything he could for you when needed, and he often delivered on that promise. My best friends and I, as we grew together, felt at times as if we had hit the friends' lottery.

Once Sticks made fun of me for having a spare refrigerator light bulb on hand because they rarely burn out (BTW, they sell them in pairs today). So my kids and I made things over the years for his wife out of refrigerator light bulbs, including an Easter basket with bulbs painted to look like eggs, complete with a story about why they were needed, as all the local chickens in a small town had taken ill. We also used refrigerator light bulbs to make various ornaments for Sticks and his family, including those for a Christmas tree. The best, though, was the necklace we made for his wife, complete with a silver chain and Tiffany-style box. She has worn it on many occasions, including to both of my daughter's weddings.

His illness came at a time we were all entering midlife— healthy, successful careers, and families we were taking care of as we raised kids. We had all experienced grief before. I am not even sure we thought of it as grief. We just knew we were sad, especially for Sticks' wife and kids.

We were not sure what to do or how to act. I say that, not meaning to sound simplistic or trite. This was just a new experience for us and, to a certain extent, hard to comprehend.

As usual, we offered to help any way we could, though Sticks and his family lived 2,000 miles away. This was before cell phones and FaceTime, so communicating with them was irregular. We often talked among ourselves on landlines and dealt with the situation each in our own private way. Periodically, we got an update from his wife.

In the end, Sticks was a great friend, one of us, so we decided our job was just to continue to be good friends. We simply wanted to act normal and help Sticks feel normal too.

Toilet Papering Houses

When we were younger, toilet papering each other's houses was a regular thing, and it became something of a game as we critiqued the quality of each other's work. Did the perpetrator cover the tops of the trees, not just the low branches? Did the toilet paper go over the roof of the house, not just hang from the edges? Was there an artistic quality to the layout?

Once, we took turns papering a house while the others judged, Olympics style, using cards with numbers one through ten. We always had fun, and as you can see, we took toilet papering seriously. Okay, okay, I made up the judging part; though, looking back, it seems as if it would have been a clever idea.

Sticks was known for the quality of his work. He acted whenever he came back to Youngstown to visit family. He papered a house and then left evidence behind, such as an article of clothing, intending to implicate someone else. As if we could not figure out it was Sticks'.

Sticks' efforts were legendary; so much so, we all promised him one day we would fly to Las Vegas and paper his house. He did not seem worried, figuring it would never happen; we were not sure either.

For that reason, one toilet-papering job stands above the rest.

Then Cancer Strikes

Sticks, along with his wife and kids, was dealing with this dreaded disease in ways we could not even imagine. The cancer was mangling his otherwise-healthy body. I remember when I asked him once what treatments the doctors prescribed.

He said, "I asked the doctors to try everything—I mean everything—radiation, chemotherapy, even things that were in a clinical-testing phase or existed in *science fiction*" (his words, not mine). He knew the score.

It was not the first time in our lives that we dealt with death. However, this was one of us, a great friend, a member of life's foundation. At times, we did not know what to think or how to act.

We came to learn how hard it is to deal with the illness of a great friend, and how helpless you feel when he lives a great distance away. We all wanted to be helpful to his wife and kids. I am sure we were in our own ways, though finding it hard at times. At this point, the rest of us had remained in the area, and we saw each other or talked on the phone regularly. You remember, the waning days of snail mail and landlines.

During the last year of Sticks' life, I was regularly traveling for business out west, therefore able to visit him once or twice a month. I saw him more in the last year of his life than in the ten years prior. I helped him eat, go to the bathroom, and dress. Such an experience changes you, usually for the better. It does make you realize how lucky you are to enjoy good health.

I know that the Hunk, the Voice, the Stud, and the Kid all felt the same way. Sticks was part of our lives.

However, to a certain extent, now we feel that our efforts were inadequate as he lay sick in a hospital bed, his wife and kids at his side, thousands of miles away, and there was little we could do but stay in touch and pray.

I do not remember many of the details of his battle. I choose at this stage to remember the good times, a method of coping that I guess is normal. Sticks did go into remission for a time, more than once, as he and his wife fought tirelessly for several years.

One year during the battle, he met us for golf in Arizona, and we did not even recognize him as he walked off the plane, his hair having regrown. However, the next year, he was unable to meet as the cancer had again struck.

I do recall a time when he returned home as the illness subsided. It gave him the chance to be with his family and sleep in his own bed. However, the prognosis was not good. His life expectancy was short. By then, the cancer had taken his eyesight.

That left us with little choice. We had to fly to Las Vegas and toilet paper his house.

Now, your reaction might be, "Toilet paper the house of a dying friend? How mean, how cruel!" The truth is our objective was to help him feel normal, to remind him we loved him. I imagine we wanted to feel normal too.

The Voice, the Hunk, the Stud, and I flew to Las Vegas to pay Sticks a visit. The Kid was unable to make the trip, but he did play a key role. Sticks was thrilled to see us. After we arrived in Las Vegas, we laid out the plan.

Needing more toilet paper than was on hand, we went shopping with the excuse that there were a few things his wife needed for dinner, though everyone except Sticks knew what we were there to buy. Sticks pushed the decoy cart cluelessly, because of his lost eyesight, as we filled a second cart with toilet paper.

His daughter, an accomplished photographer, took pictures the entire day, from the time of our arrival in Las Vegas until the climax, creating priceless photos that are now cherished treasures.

Upon returning to his house, we headed to the backyard and piled the toilet paper in the shape of a pyramid on the patio table. We talked and laughed for a while, then got to work as his daughter continued to click away.

We proceeded to paper the backyard and rear of the house. It was a large house on a golf course in a newer section of Las Vegas, north of the Strip. What we were about to do was not something the neighbors were accustomed to seeing. We figured he would be in big trouble with the homeowners association; Sticks had received just that day a notice because his exterior garage light had burned out. This was a bit different.

We all sat on the back patio, talking and laughing, as we clandestinely took turns papering the back of the house and yard, including trees and bushes; you could see the mountains in the background. We decided to skip the front of the house, as setting up our dying friend to answer to the HOA was not part of the plan.

Sticks was unaware, as we were careful not to talk close to him; we assumed it is true that when you lose your eyesight, it sharpens your hearing. This was a smart guy; he might get suspicious if he thought we were up to something.

In the end, it was an amateurish quality of work, as we did not want to make too big of a scene. We were there because we loved him, not to earn an Olympics score of ten. Upon completion, we posed with Sticks, enabling his daughter to get just the right photo as we were about to let the cat out of the bag.

The Stud answered when the Kid called. He handed the phone to Sticks. The Kid told Sticks he was sorry for not joining us, but that he had enjoyed the photos the Stud had texted him (yes, texting photos was now possible), that he thought Sticks' home was beautiful, especially the view out the back towards the mountains. However, the Kid explained, he had never seen decorations quite like Sticks'.

Sticks asked, "What do you mean?"

The Kid said, "Your decorations, they are unique." When Sticks again asked the Kid what he meant, the Kid answered, "Ask the Stud."

Upon doing so, the Stud handed Sticks a roll of toilet paper.

Sticks then said, "Let me see if I have this right. I am blind and dying, and you guys toilet papered my house?"

"Yes, of course," we answered, reminding him we promised to do so one day.

The photo his daughter took at that moment has a place of honor in each of our homes.

Moments later, Sticks' sprinkler system, which was on an automatic timer, came on. We were not used to such high technology; we marveled at it as we watched the water soak the bushes and trees adorned by the toilet paper. Surprised, we quickly retrieved the toilet paper, not needing to keep quiet as the gig was up.

If only for a short while, I am quite sure Sticks felt normal. I know we did.

Goodbye, Old Friend

Sticks died a brief time thereafter. Many attended the celebration of life and demonstrated their love for Sticks. Friends and family from Youngstown, Las Vegas, and elsewhere were there.

We all attended his celebration of life in Las Vegas; both a sad and happy occasion not to be missed. We met a few of his local friends whom we had heard about over the years. The Stud and the Voice spoke, outlining the top-ten memories from our friendships. What do you suppose was at the top of the list?

When I was married, I had a photo taken of the six of us standing in a semicircle, each holding a raised shot glass, about to make a toast. Twenty-five years later, at Sticks' funeral, we recreated the photo, his son standing in for him. And at my daughter's wedding, fifteen years after that, the photo features Sticks' wife in his place. Enduring symbols of how much these friendships mean to all of us.

We gathered back at the house afterwards. Walking out to the nearby golf tee, carrying his ashes with us, we took turns hitting golf balls left-handed (a few of us, not well) and reminiscing. You guessed it, Sticks played golf left-handed.

After the gathering, the Hunk got up to leave and head to the airport. As we all said our goodbyes, he looked for his shoes but could not find them. He asked if anyone had seen his shoes.

Of course, we knew by the look on his face he already knew the answer as someone yelled out, "Check the freezer."

Epilogue

At the time, we all knew this was the end of a chapter and the start of a new one. We also knew the story of Sticks and these friendships would last forever. So they have.

My daughters and I had dinner with Sticks' wife recently in Las Vegas. We spent the time reminiscing and telling stories that get better over time. Yes, of course, his wife was wearing the Tiffany-style refrigerator-light-bulb necklace.

Sticks' wife has papered a few houses in Youngstown over the years following Sticks' passing. In fact, a few years ago, I papered the Kid's house after she encouraged me to do so, having spoken to her earlier in the day.

We all remain close friends. I trust we always will. In fact, the Voice helped conspire to hide my shoes in the Stud's freezer just last year when a good friend and I visited. Old traditions die hard.

*To Dad—Jack Lopes. A father, an uncle,
a brother, a son, a smart businessman, a mentor,
a friend, an author, a beacon, a rock. My rock.*

Losing Dad

Diane Lopes

It was a Friday evening in late spring. The kind of day that was unusually warm and gave glimpses of the summer months ahead. I was deep in thought, contemplating what to make the kids for dinner or whether to order takeout. My phone on the table startled me when it rang; I looked and saw it was Dad calling. It was odd for him to call on a Friday evening but I always welcomed our conversations.

When I picked up, his voice was strained, shaky, but direct. "I need to go to the hospital. Please come over."

My feet hit the floor, I grabbed the keys, and I was out the door in minutes. I called my brother as I drove, my heart racing; I felt a warm flush come over my body. For Dad to call and say this, I knew it was serious. This was the man who, years earlier, left a message on my voicemail saying he "had a heart flutter" and "would be away a few days to take care of it." He was in Florida; I was in Connecticut. The heart flutter was a heart attack, and he was in the hospital having bypass surgery.

Dad was upstairs in bed when I arrived at his place. By the look on his face, I knew he was in agonizing pain. His usual beautiful olive complexion was pale gray. He couldn't get up or even move. I called 911 as my brother arrived.

The emergency-response team quickly got Dad onto a special chair to take him down the stairs and out the door to the ambulance. The pained look on his face was one I had never seen, nor will I ever forget it. In the years since, I have tried to erase that image from my memory to no avail.

I followed the ambulance to the hospital emergency room. My knuckles went white from my tight grip on the steering wheel, and I had to force myself to remember to breathe.

At the hospital, they determined Dad was in septic shock and needed to be transported immediately to a larger hospital. Dad had perforated diverticulitis and was very sick. The next few days were a blur as my brother and I rotated going to the hospital, talking to doctors, and determining the plan for surgery, treatment, rehab, and recovery. We almost lost him, but true to Dad's style, with grit and tenacity, he bounced back. Like a cat, he had nine lives. I had lost count, but at this point, he was probably down to six lives. This wasn't the first time Dad had a medical crisis that gave us a scare and made us think we'd lose him.

Dad was in the hospital for about two weeks following major intestinal surgery. He did not do well with anesthesia and had episodes of hallucinations that were terrifying. He also wasn't a good patient. Always a strong, independent man, Dad didn't like others caring for him. I love him dearly, but *belligerent* may be the right word for how he conducted himself. It pained me to see him like that because I knew him so well, but I also knew he needed to be in the hospital to heal and recover. At this point, I began to realize that things would never be the same.

Dad was discharged to a skilled-nursing facility. It was expected he'd be there for several weeks. He was now using a wheelchair, and he'd need extensive physical therapy to get back on his feet. Dad was a gregarious man, and his affability was infectious, but he also valued his privacy. To say he hated the facility is an understatement. He had a roommate and had to share a bathroom.

He would cocoon himself by pulling the curtain all the way around his bed tightly. It reminded me of the tents we'd make as kids with sheets and couch cushions—a bittersweet memory, as I had pangs of regret for not appreciating those carefree days as much as I missed them now.

Dad constantly asked to be discharged, saying he didn't need to be there. He said everyone there was "old and almost dead"; he saw himself as young and vibrant, so did I. It broke my heart, but also made me laugh a bit. Dad never looked or acted his age, and he could be a stubborn guy. It was that stubborn side that had him resisting all physical therapy. Again, he was borderline belligerent, but in the most respectful way toward the staff. A natural flirt, Dad loved to tease the staff and have fun. These were sparks of his old self. He once introduced one of his aides to me as my future stepmother.

Unfortunately, Dad never got back on his feet and the wheelchair became a permanent fixture in our lives. When he was discharged from the skilled-nursing facility, we had to move him into an apartment that was all on one level and wheelchair accessible. He couldn't go back to his condo as the bedroom and bathroom were on the second floor, and laundry was in the basement. He loved that condo, and it broke me to tell him he couldn't go back there.

Dad was at the apartment for only six days. We hired visiting nurses and personal aides, but Dad got pneumonia and went back into the hospital. After another lengthy inpatient stay, he was discharged again to the skilled-nursing facility. I knew in my heart that he would not be able to leave the facility this time. He was there to stay.

For as far back as I can remember, Dad forgot words or used the wrong ones. He used to buy me wine coolers and called them Broccoli & Jaymes (instead of Bartles & Jaymes). He always forgot peoples' names, and I had to remind him; we did it stealthily as I whispered in his ear. I thought this was the normal aging process, even though it probably started when he was in his fifties, the age I am now.

In the facility, Dad's memory deteriorated rapidly; he forgot significant life events, and his short-term memories escaped him. He often blamed it on his hearing aids, saying he couldn't hear what people were saying. This became a frustrating circle of dialogue—his hearing aids "not functioning." My brother and I got his hearing aids cleaned and adjusted, we repeatedly replaced the batteries, but he still claimed he couldn't hear. It was frustrating for all of us, but even worse, it was heartbreaking. In a desperate attempt to help him hear the correct words, we bought him brand-new hearing aids, which were customized following extensive hearing tests. Nothing helped. Dad continued to say he didn't hear the words. In reality, he heard the words; he just no longer understood them.

Slowly, day by day, Dad faded away. He would occasionally surprise us with a random story that he'd remember. He'd look at his high school yearbook and remember stories about his classmates, but the short-term memories vanished as they happened. Dad was often frustrated and angry, moods that I rarely had seen him display in the past. I knew he didn't want to be in the facility with no autonomy or independence. The wheelchair was a blessing and a curse as it kept him mobile but trapped at the same time.

I remember a conversation Dad and I had twenty-plus years prior. He said if he ever got to the point that he needed to live in a facility, he did not want to continue living. He agonized over the fact that he had to move his own beloved mother into one of those nursing homes, and he hated every minute of it. He never wanted that for himself or for us to have to force him into one. At that dinner table so many years before, during the conversation we had over a great dinner and bottle of white wine, he told me he'd rather be dead than live in that situation. He asked me to shoot him if it ever came to that. Yes, shoot him. We laughed, but then he got serious; apparently, he had a plan. He'd get a gun and keep it in a desk drawer for me to use if necessary. He told me that he knew I had it in me to fulfill this final request.

I didn't know if I should be honored or horrified. Shoot him!? Certainly, that wasn't something I could do, legally or emotionally. Seeing him in that facility and knowing his wishes, my heart broke more and more with each visit. There he was, in a facility and in that wheelchair, exactly like his own mother. I felt as if I had let him down.

Dementia and aphasia took Dad from us. It seemed gradual, increasing over many years, but also it felt as if it had occurred in the blink of an eye. Physically, he was there, but mentally he wasn't. I found myself torn between gratitude that he was physically with me and guilt knowing that he didn't want to live that way, but there was nothing I could do. I also realized that my grief had begun long before his death, while he was still present on this earth.

As an adult, I've spent a good amount of time reflecting on my childhood and my relationship with my Dad. When I was very young, Dad traveled extensively for work. His job provided him with a window to the world, literally and figuratively. I was too young to understand where he was specifically; I just knew that he wasn't home, and I missed him. When he returned from those trips, he always brought me a surprise, usually a stuffed animal. They would spark my imagination as to where Dad had been.

Once, it was a stuffed dog dressed as an English bobby, what the British call their police officers. I imagined Dad walking the cobblestone streets of London, searching for the perfect toy store to get me this most treasured gift. There was also a stuffed husky. I imagined Dad had gotten him in a snowy, mountainous country. One where people wore big, furry coats, boots up to their knees, and scarves wrapped around their red faces. As much as I hated him being away from home, I loved his return with these magical gifts. These stories filled my head for days and weeks, until Dad left on his next trip.

When I went to college, Dad moved to Florida for a new job opportunity. He seemed to love his new job, he loved Florida, and he met an amazing woman who joined our lives for decades to come. He was the happiest I had ever seen him. I was happy that he was happy. I felt that I had matured to the point that I could see a genuine ease and joy in him. Maybe he had moments of joy before that, but I don't think he was completely consumed with a sense of peace in his life until he moved to Florida.

We traveled back and forth and had wonderful visits and adventures. Dad and I always called our times together "shenanigans." Dad and I always had an unspoken connection. We'd make eye contact and just start laughing. Sometimes, it was at other people's expense, such as a person in the grocery store arguing with the butcher about the cut of meat (why was she so angry over pot roast?), or the time his employees went on strike and made a dummy of his likeness and hung it from a tree. I suggested we buy the strikers coffee and doughnuts because they were walking in circles in the frigid weather. These were people I had met many times at Dad's office and at company picnics. I didn't understand what "going on strike" meant. I just knew that I liked many of the people striking; they were always kind to me. Dad appreciated them and their right to strike as well, so he happily granted my request, and we bought them the coffee and doughnuts. It wasn't until my adult life that I realized how odd that must have seemed to these striking employees. Then again, they knew Dad and that he truly respected and supported them, so maybe they weren't surprised.

With Dad in Florida and me in Connecticut, we talked every Sunday morning. Sometimes, we talked for hours. He was eager and excited to hear about my new job after college and the progression in my career. I had started in an entry-level job at a big insurance company and received several promotions in my first couple of years. Dad was my career guide, mentor, advisor, and biggest fan. We bonded in an entirely new way. And new shenanigans. We laughed about my silly work stories and my dealings with customers, peers, and managers. And he shared more and more work-related stories with me.

Many stories were about those trips he used to take all over the world. It was fascinating to replace my childhood imaginary versions of his travels with reality. And reality was far beyond anything I could have imagined.

He told me stories of Turkey, Haiti, Israel, Germany, and other Eastern European countries. The people he met, the endeavors he took on, the work he did supporting underserved communities across the world. He was truly an impressive man.

I began traveling for work, which felt like a full-circle moments, as I was traveling as he had. On my trips, I got to know the airport gift shops. They had all the things a weary traveler needed. I had gotten married and had two daughters at this point, so I would buy them trinkets and toys in these shops. One day I had a realization. Did Dad buy all those stuffed animals in airport gift shops? My thoughts of him searching for hours for the perfect shop on cobblestone streets lined with gas lanterns to find me the perfect gift burst like a bubble. Poof!!

With the clarity of adult understanding, I felt mixed emotions, but mostly I chuckled to myself. It's amazing that parents can do something so simple, yet thoughtful, to brighten their child's day. It helped me understand Dad more, and I appreciated that he even thought of a gift when he was most likely tired and in a rush to catch a flight home. He could have easily passed by the gift ship without a second thought, but he didn't.

Dad passed away in the overnight hours of October 8, 2022. I left the nursing facility before dawn and headed home. The predawn darkness perfectly hid my tears and allowed me an escape from reality. Somehow, the sun rising didn't feel right. How could a new day dawn without my Dad on this earth. I raced home to crawl into bed before the light could shine on the sad reality that life goes on even after one amazing life ends.

In the days following Dad's passing, I found myself becoming puzzled, even annoyed, at seeing people going about their daily lives. They were grocery shopping, doing yard work, attending sporting events, jogging—things I didn't pay attention to before Dad died, but now they seemed out of place. The sun came up, and it set...again and again. But now my world had stopped, and I felt as if everyone else's world should stop too. Didn't they realize we lost the greatest man who walked the earth? I know; this sounds overdramatic, but it's how I felt.

I was also overwhelmed with a feeling of guilt. I didn't spend enough time with him. How did I not realize that one day he would be gone? I was upset with myself for taking for granted that he was always there. When my basement flooded, he came with a wet vac and spent hours dumping the water outside. When we got a puppy who needed daily walks, he was there. When I had a terrible kidney infection and needed to go to the emergency room, he drove me and sat with me for thirteen hours in the waiting room. When my kids had a sports game or a dance recital, he was there cheering them on.

He was unassuming, so very proud, and so very present. Now, he was gone. I would never again see him in the distance, waving with his whole body so that I could see him—the way he did when picking me up at the airport and when he arrived anywhere. As a teenager, it embarrassed me. His right arm extended fully above his head; stretching to see over the crowd and exuberantly waving. As an adult, it was a welcome sight that brought me comfort and peace. A sight that I will miss for the rest of my life.

*In Memory of Malka Susana Lina
and Lloyd Joel Mankes*

Echoes of Love

Navigating Grief, Finding Resilience,
Happiness, and Renewed Hope

Dr. Carol Leibovich-Mankes, DrOT, OTR/L, PLCC, GC-C

Introduction

I view my life as a narrative, similar to a storybook. Every chapter, some of which I'll be sharing in the next few pages, has been filled with blessings, challenges, experiences, relationships, and pivotal events that have shaped the person I am today. Upon contemplation, I noticed that recurrent themes of grief and loss—steered by faith and encountered with resilience, hope, and the pursuit of happiness—are part of my journey. These repeating occurrences have taught me the importance of embracing vulnerability and finding strength in adversity. They have also deepened my appreciation for the power of resilience and the ability to overcome obstacles, which ultimately leads to personal growth, transformation, and healing.

My life story not only encompasses moments of joy and valuable lessons but also confronts the harsh realities of financial instability, immigration, divorce, infertility, shuttered dreams, and loss. All of these have led to a shared journey akin to a grief process. I had to navigate the emotional complexities, uncertainties, and adjustments associated with each unique struggle.

In the face of these numerous challenges, I've consistently chosen not to give up. Instead, I've opted to transform life's difficulties into opportunities. Recognizing that I cannot entirely control the past, present, and future, as those aspects lie in God's hands, however, I can control my daily approach. I have turned every challenge into an opportunity to initiate new chapters filled with hope and gratitude. Embracing a mindset of resilience and adaptability, I have learned to uncover silver linings in every situation, regardless of its difficulty. Through persistent effort and self-reflection, I have navigated life's storms and emerged with increased strength, compassion, and determination to seize the fullest potential of every moment.

In sharing these chapters of my life, I intend to guide and empower each reader to navigate grief and loss with resilience and hope. Grief and loss can be catalysts for growth, healing, and empowerment as we recognize that we have the power to shape our stories despite the challenges we encounter. By embracing our emotions and finding healthy coping mechanisms, we can transform our pain into strength and find meaning in despair. It is through these shared experiences that we inspire others to embrace their journeys of healing and discover the resilience within themselves.

Life-Altering Events Inducing Facets of Grief and Loss

Grief across Borders: Navigating the Immigration Journey and Parents' Divorce

At the age of twelve, a pivotal chapter unfolded in my life and marked my initial encounter with the journey of grief. This grief was intricately tied to the act of leaving my homeland, Israel, and embarking on the journey of emigration to the USA, which was a significant, profound, and transformative shift. Emigrating to a new country can be likened to a grief process, as it involves bidding farewell to the familiar, navigating uncertainties, and adapting to an entirely different way of life.

Navigating adolescence is inherently challenging; coupling that with the complexities of adapting to a new country, learning a different language, and assimilating into a foreign culture made the journey monumentally difficult. The familiar landscapes of Israel gave way to the unfamiliar streets of a new land. The language, Hebrew, I used to hear every day was replaced by English, a language that was initially unfamiliar and intimidating.

This relocation wasn't merely about adjusting to a new culture; it introduced a different kind of uncertainty— the constant worry of deportation. The sense of security and familiarity to which I was accustomed suddenly vanished. In their place were constant instability and continuous awareness of being an immigrant. The toll on my family was profound.

Navigating a new life strained my parents' marriage to the point of dissolution. The once-unified family structure unraveled, and when faced with challenges beyond what they'd anticipated, my parents decided to part ways. The dissolution of our family unit was life-altering. Grief, a constant companion, settled in as I grappled with the loss of what I had known. Family dinners, shared laughter, and unity gave way to solitude. The dynamics I previously took for granted were replaced by a fragmented reality, and the feeling of loss was deep.

But even though this chapter was transformative and painful, it gave me a deeper understanding of myself. Through the pain and grief, I discovered strength within me that I never knew existed. As I navigated this new reality, I learned to rely on my resilience and adaptability.

It was a bittersweet realization that sometimes growth comes from the most challenging circumstances.

Fertility's Trials: A Journey of Resilience, Grief, and Joy

Moving forward in life, the next significant chapter further developed my relationship with grief, as it unfolded after my high school sweetheart, Lloyd Mankes, and I began our married life armed with dreams and aspirations. I pursued a doctorate in occupational therapy, while he dedicated himself to law school. Together, we were scripting the story of our shared future.

As we embraced the prospect of expanding our family, an unexpected and arduous challenge awaited—a five-year struggle with infertility—which introduced an element of grief into our marriage. The emotional toll of infertility resonated daily, impacting not only our well-being but also the dynamics of our relationship. We confronted the stark reality of unfulfilled dreams and the persistent ache of longing for a child. Each failed attempt brought a layer of grief intertwined with the uncertainty of whether our dreams would ever materialize, which added emotional weight to our journey.

After numerous attempts, various infertility treatments, and significant financial investment, hope prevailed, and our prayers were answered. The arrival of our beautiful daughter, Arielle, brought immeasurable joy and marked the end of our infertility journey. It seemed as if life was finally aligning with our dreams. We had the family and stability we had wished for, and we were anticipating a future characterized by ease and tranquility.

Amid the challenges and emotional turbulence, we discovered resilience and strength. We learned to lean on each other for support and acknowledge that our shared journey through infertility was shaping us in ways we hadn't anticipated. The grief became a poignant presence, a reminder of the profound desire for a family and the resilience required to confront the unexpected twists on our path.

Grief amid Learning Differences

The subsequent significant chapter in my life unfolded when the birth of my daughter brought forth another dimension of grief—this time linked to navigating the intricacies of her learning differences. Like most parents, we had high hopes for our child's future, ones that followed the typical paths defined by social norms and milestones.

Despite the joy of having a healthy girl, we swiftly realized that our daughter's unique journey required an adjustment of those expectations. The conventional narrative of academic benchmarks and standard achievements had to shift and make room for a new definition of success—one that embraced individual strengths, celebrated small victories, and cultivated an environment that nurtured personal growth.

This process of adjustment wasn't without its challenges; it necessitated a recalibration of dreams and the cultivation of resilience in the face of societal pressures. In this journey, grief and loss weren't end points, but rather an ongoing process while adapting to new narratives and appreciating the inherent worth and beauty of neurodiversity. Through the lens of grief, we discovered that adjusting expectations wasn't a concession, but a powerful act of embracing the uniqueness of our daughter's path. This realization prompted a thorough exploration of her unique strengths and challenges.

Navigating the educational landscape transformed into an adventure of its own. We found ourselves passionately advocating for her needs, working collaboratively with teachers, and delving into innovative approaches to learning. Observing her resilience and determination in the face of challenges has been a source of profound humility and inspiration. This experience became a transformative chapter that not only reshaped our understanding of parenthood but also illuminated the strength derived from navigating uncharted territories with an open heart and an unwavering commitment to our child's well-being and happiness.

This journey of acceptance and growth has imparted the importance of celebrating small victories and finding joy in the present moment, rather than dwelling on what could have been. Ultimately, embracing reality has enriched our lives and allowed us to see the world through a new lens filled with compassion, understanding, and endless possibilities for our daughter's future.

Navigating the Depths of Grief: Confronting Dual Losses

My previous struggles were nothing compared to what awaited me in the next chapter, which was characterized by grief due to a devastating loss. This time, grief revealed itself in its truest, most agonizing form. In 2016, both my mother and husband were simultaneously diagnosed with cancer. This marked the beginning of a challenging period in which I found myself rushing from one hospital to another, tirelessly fighting for their lives.

While balancing this intense emotional struggle, I had to make critical decisions while maintaining a full-time job and attempting to provide a sense of normalcy for my daughter. Tragically, in just three weeks, both my mother and husband succumbed to cancer. It felt as though an unbearable weight had been placed on my shoulders, and the simultaneous departure of these two pillars in my life propelled me into a tumultuous whirlwind of emotions—grief, anger, and confusion. Each crashing wave threatened to engulf me with overwhelming force.

Grieving one loss would have been formidable, but facing the dual void seemed insurmountable.

Initially, the path through grief appeared shrouded in impenetrable darkness, each step a strenuous struggle, and the weight of sorrow threatened to pull me into its abyss. I found myself a single mom and a widow at forty-three. What was I to do? After overcoming numerous challenges in the past, it was difficult to fathom that I now faced a task that appeared to be as daunting as climbing Mount Everest.

Yet, within this darkness, I could perceive the outlines of resilience. Thinking back to the mountains I had previously climbed, I was confident that I could do it again because of my tenacity and faith in God. I came to understand that grief doesn't follow a straight path; it's more like a roller coaster with unexpected twists and turns. Grief requires both patience and courage. Upon reaching this realization, I made a conscious choice to ride out the tumultuous waves of grief and confront the pain head-on.

After making this choice, I sought to cultivate inner strength, foster perseverance, and nurture a sense of hope not only for myself, but also for my daughter, to guide us toward a brighter future. I decided once again that my new, unexplainable circumstances were not going to define me. I made a conscious decision to gather all my strength and life lessons and fight like a lion.

While grieving for my mom and husband, I needed to rebuild both my life and that of my daughter. I had to build a solid new foundation and find a new livelihood (being now the sole provider), be a solo mom, and move forward the best I could. I chose to be a warrior, not a victim.

Embarking on this healing journey, I solemnly dedicated myself to honoring the cherished memories of my beloved mother and husband; both left indelible imprints on my life. I reminded myself that their purpose while alive was to ensure my success and happiness, and I committed to keeping their flame alive. Their absence served as a constant reminder of the strength and resilience they had instilled in me. Embracing their legacy, I channeled the enduring flame of their love into fuel for my determination to create a brighter future for both my daughter and me.

Navigating Grief: Embracing Divine Timing and Enduring Love

As the seventh anniversary of the profound loss of my mom and husband approaches, the chance to share my experiences through writing this chapter has emerged. This serendipitous moment aligns with a day meant to honor what would have been my mother's birthday, December 12, and the week leading up to what would have been my wedding anniversary, December 17.

The timing of this unexpected opportunity adds a profound layer to the beliefs and convictions that have guided me throughout my life and assisted me in navigating the journey of grief. I've always held the steadfast belief that life unfolds as it's meant for each of us—not to bring a person down, but to build that person up. The secret is to be open and aware enough to accept the signs from above. Central to my journey has always been a steadfast belief in God's divine plan and the conviction that my life unfolds with a purpose meticulously tailored for me. This conviction holds even in the face of circumstances as incomprehensible as the ones I have encountered.

Embracing this belief led me to recognize that the fulfillment of both my daughter's and my distinct destinies necessitates not only acknowledging and contemplating our experiences but also striving to understand the profound lessons presented by the dear people we lost. Anchored in unwavering faith, this journey is a testament to the resilience of the human spirit, the power of belief, and the enduring impact of love, even in the shadow of profound loss.

Through this journey, I have come to understand that our loved ones never truly leave us, but instead they continue to guide and inspire us from beyond. Their presence is felt in the smallest of moments as they remind us to cherish every breath and embrace the beauty of life. This realization has given me the strength to carry on, knowing that their love will forever be a part of my daughter's and my unique paths.

Loss of My Loved Ones

Loss of a Mother: Malka Susana Lina

My mother, Malka Susana Lina, was born in Buenos Aires, Argentina, in 1952. She was a pillar of love characterized by the spirit of giving, unconditional affection, unwavering trust, and unparalleled support. Despite life's challenges, her legacy endures in the valuable lessons she passed on and the well of inspiration she provided. Her journey, from childhood dreams in Argentina to her role as a devoted mother in the USA, unfolded with threads of resilience, determination, and sacrifice.

At the age of ten, my mom moved with her family to Israel; she carried aspirations of becoming an artist and eventually emigrating to the USA to work for Disney. She attended a prestigious art school in Israel and secured a scholarship to study in France. However, life took her in a different direction. At nineteen, she embraced marriage and motherhood, and she eventually became a loving mother to my two brothers and me.

A courageous step at the age of thirty-two led my mom to uproot her family and move to the USA, pursuing the American dream and her longtime dream of being an accomplished artist. Despite the challenges that punctuated her life, my mom's journey was a testament to her resilience, determination, and the sacrifices she made for the well-being of our family. Her story mirrored the optimistic immigrant narrative filled with hopes and dreams and the persistent pursuit of a better life for her family. A woman of tenacity and ambition, she became a cornerstone of hard work, epitomizing the immigrant spirit. My mom's experience in the United States was characterized by her holding various jobs as she tirelessly pursued a dream she had nurtured since childhood. As always, her path took twists and turns, but she was determined to reach her lifelong goals.

As she navigated her journey, her entrepreneurial spirit blossomed and led her to establish a successful beauty salon that became more than just a business—it symbolized stability for our family for over two decades. However, my mom remained determined to fulfill her dream of becoming an artist.

Approximately five years before her untimely illness, she decided to retire and reignite her passion for the arts. During this period, she created stunning artwork that proudly adorns my living room today. Her creations spanned both traditional and nontraditional art, including three-dimensional pieces showcasing her innovative approach before it became widely popular. She was on the verge of redefining her life and achieving her goal when illness struck suddenly and claimed her.

Her absence, particularly on significant days like her birthday or Mother's Day, is a lasting burden. Those days heighten the longing, sorrow, and deep sense of missing her. Yet, amid grief, I've found comfort and strength in holding on to the vivid memories and reflecting on the precious times we shared. The process of recognizing and contemplating these experiences has been a poignant and transformative one. In recalling her laughter and the warmth of her embrace, I've discovered profound lessons that go beyond the confines of grief. It's a journey of understanding—not just the depth of loss but also the lasting impact that love and resilience can have on the human spirit.

My mom's legacy reaches far beyond her lifetime; it's an enduring influence that guides me. It embodies resilience, love, and the lasting impact of a mother's advice. This acknowledgment empowers me to face life's challenges with determination. Leveraging her entrepreneurial drive, I've crafted a successful legacy as a pediatric occupational therapist, parent coach, and grief counselor, embodying the spirit inherited from my mom. My recently released book is more than just a personal achievement; it stands as a powerful testament to my mother's unshakable belief in my abilities and my potential to reach great heights.

My mom's life serves as a poignant example of a journey intricately intertwined with a broader narrative of love, sacrifice, and the timeless pursuit of a better life.

It inspires my daughter and me to embrace these values and shape our choices for generations to come.

Loss of a Spouse: Lloyd Joel Mankes

My late husband, Lloyd Joel Mankes, was born in Florida, USA, in 1970, and he passed away at the tender age of forty-five as we celebrated twenty-one years of marriage. Our journey began in high school, and after four years of dating, we embarked on a journey filled with love and excitement to build a home together. We exchanged vows on December 17, 1995.

Despite being two very different people, we found inspiration in each other and pushed each other to reach our goals. Lloyd, a daring and tenacious spirit, lived life boldly. While he projected a tough exterior to those he met, his close friends knew him as a gentle, caring man always ready to go the extra mile for his loved ones. In 1998, he realized his childhood dream of becoming a criminal defense attorney, eventually becoming the president of the Broward Association of Criminal Defense Lawyers. His passion for advocacy was not just a profession but a commitment to justice and the well-being of his clients.

Throughout our twenty-five years together, we faced various challenges, including a five-year battle with infertility. Despite the difficulties, our resilience defied the odds. In 2006, the joyous occasion of fatherhood unfolded as Lloyd embraced the role of a dedicated and loving father to our daughter, Arielle. This new addition to our family brought immeasurable joy and added profound meaning to our lives. Lloyd's commitment as a father was truly remarkable, as he invested his heart and soul into cherishing Arielle. His purpose extended beyond the ordinary responsibilities of parenthood; he aimed to create a collection of beautiful memories that would resonate with warmth and love throughout Arielle's life. Every moment spent together became an opportunity for Lloyd to impart not just care but a sense of security, joy, and profound connection. Through his unwavering commitment, he shaped a legacy of love that left an indelible mark on Arielle's heart and enriched our family with a treasure trove of cherished moments; his legacy will endure.

Losing my spouse was a profound and life-altering experience that took me on a complex journey through a spectrum of intense emotions—from the deep ache of grief to the unsettling waves of loneliness that accompany the absence of a life partner. Beyond the emotional toll, this loss permeated every facet of my existence, touched on the practical aspects of daily life, and shook my fundamental sense of identity and purpose.

The loss of my spouse, combined with the simultaneous role of becoming a solo mom, thrust me into an alternate reality—a realm where the familiar was suddenly off-balance without the person who was always there. The weight of responsibilities became heavier as I attempted to navigate through a void of emptiness and shattered dreams. It's an inexplicable journey to become a solo parent, akin to entering uncharted territory with only memories of the past and crushing uncertainties about what lies ahead.

The impact was not confined only to me; it extended to my daughter. In the immediate aftermath of her father's passing, my daughter, age ten, confronted a whirlwind of emotions. As her mother, it fell upon me to deliver the heartbreaking news. I made a crucial decision to allow her to visit the hospital and bid farewell to her father. Though her dad was already in a deep coma, the belief persisted that he waited for her visit to finally let go. This decision aimed to offer some semblance of closure and prepare her for the devastating truth that followed.

The realization that her dad was no longer physically present brought forth a tidal wave of sorrow, anger, and frustration for my daughter. The unfairness of losing her father at such a tender age and the dreams and milestones they would never share stirred a fiery storm within me as her mother. Yet, amidst the pain, my unwavering promise as her mother was to stand by, comfort, and support her through this intricate and multifaceted process.

It's a delicate dance between mourning for myself and providing comfort to my daughter as she navigates her unique pain. This dance requires immense strength and resilience as we navigate the unpredictable waves of grief and strive to find meaning amid loss. It is a process that demands vulnerability, courage, and an intricate interplay of memory and healing. Each day brings new layers to this already complex experience.

Conclusion

This chapter, which unfolds as a narrative of my life, is a storybook filled with highs and lows in which grief and loss take center stage. However, amid the somber notes, an inner strength emerges, propelling me forward in the continued pursuit of happiness. My journey stands as a testament to human resilience, and it emphasizes the intentional choice to live joyfully despite the challenges.

Harnessing loss as a driving force for progress has become a crucial aspect of my understanding. I've grown to embrace the idea that progressing and finding happiness aren't betrayals of grief, but rather testaments to the complexity of our human experience.

Gratitude has become my compass; it guides me to be present in every moment and to celebrate life's small miracles. I am dedicated to the continual process of gaining insights from life experiences and lessons from loved ones I've lost. These have transformed me as I navigate through diverse situations and challenges.

Looking back on this journey, I see a story of love surpassing time and mortality. In the intertwined dance of grief and joy, my mother and late husband persist in their influence; they have extended beyond their physical presence to become enduring guides for my daughter and me. My aim is not merely to confront life's challenges, but to do so with the love and strength inherited from them. I will create a legacy of love, sacrifice, and pursuit of a better life.

To those grappling with grief and the healing process, I offer a reminder not to be too hard on yourselves. Grief is a journey, not a destination; it's ongoing and personal. No one can dictate what you should feel, when, or how. Yet I encourage readers to commit to finding resilience, renewed happiness, and, above all, a life that honors the enduring echoes of love.

In Memory of
Daria Switankowsky

Memories of
My Late Mama

Irene S. Roth

1 have so many memories of my mama, and I miss her so much. She passed away in March of 2011. And every March, before my birthday on the seventeenth, I recall how she used to call me to wish me a happy birthday and cry. She always cried on my birthday.

Now, many years after her death, I still cry on my birthday when I remember how emotional she was. There were always stories about how I was born during the St. Patrick's Day parade at two o'clock in the afternoon and how she was so happy to have me in her arms.

Then there were the stories of how I was famous when the hospital asked her if I could be in a baby-food commercial. She was so proud of that and always reminded me of how beautiful I was.

As I grew up, I felt very smothered by her love. At first, it was really wonderful to get all that attention. Because my mother had difficult pregnancies, I was an only child. She did try to have more children, but she kept miscarrying. In fact, I came after all these miscarriages. To be sure all would go well while she was carrying me, my mama had to quit her job and go on complete bed rest from the second trimester onwards to make sure that she didn't miscarry again.

Being an only child had a lot of perks, but also quite a few drawbacks. I had all the attention and love. My parents knew how to love and dote on me. So I got a lot of gifts at Christmas and on birthdays.

However, they didn't spoil me. They were able to say no, and when they said no, they meant it. My mama was the disciplinarian. There were times that her comments towards me were quite harsh. But despite being hurt, I always believed that she loved me. And she taught me a lot of valuable lessons during these times.

But not having any siblings or extended family made me very lonely at times. I remember sitting in my room and feeling so desperately alone. Also, because my mama was an immigrant and didn't speak English fluently, we didn't have a lot of people over to visit. She felt like an outsider, even among our neighbors.

Even when we went to church, she felt out of place and never reached out to any of the ladies there. They tried to be friendly towards her, and they all liked me a lot and called me a beautiful girl. But my mama was still very suspicious of them. So, again, I felt alone.

Our holidays were times of peace and quiet. There were just the three of us. I enjoyed the Christmas holidays, as my mama baked and cooked for a week before the big day. She baked her own bread, cakes, and shortbread cookies. I helped her. We used to put on Christmas carols while we cooked and baked. Sometimes, we'd sing along with them.

A few days before Christmas, we'd go to the delicatessen close to our home and pick up what seemed like a lot of deli meat and cherry strudel. I loved going to the delicatessen because it smelled so good. And everyone in the store seemed so happy and kind. It was certainly a time of great joy and jubilation. I couldn't wipe the smile off my face.

Then, my mama made all of her furniture covers and decorations for our home. We had a real Christmas tree.

The aromas of pine and spruce, depending on the year, wafted through the house. My tata always went to a tree farm close to where we lived and cut down his own tree. It was such a wonderful time of year. Many times, my mama and I accompanied him.

But I was still quite lonely. I started even feeling like a bit of a loner. I'd spend hours by myself in my room, reading, writing, and journaling. I'd even make my own crafts, sew homemade dolls, and make tiny furniture covers with my own small sewing machine.

I also loved crocheting. My mama always had a lot of different yarns to choose from. She taught me from a very early age how to knit and crochet. I started making some clothes for my Barbie and quickly progressed to making scarves for the Salvation Army. When I was sixteen, I started making socks for the homeless, as well as mitts and baby blankets.

So I had a lot of things to do. But I was still lonely. I craved having deep friendships with girls my own age. I wanted to be able to go out with people my own age. I even made up friends in my imagination so that I wouldn't feel so lonely.

Yet those years were some of the best times of my life; they formed the fabric of my life as it is now. Although

I have friends now, I still crave solitude. I am an introvert, and I love being on my own at least some of the time.

I really believe that if I hadn't spent so much time alone when I was a young girl and a teenager, I wouldn't be the writer or the person I am today. I also wouldn't have patience with my students and compassion to offer.

The other memory I have of my mama is her kindness. She was kind, not only towards me and my tata, but towards everyone she met. Even when my mama met strangers, she always reached out to them with an unquenchable love and kindness.

Because it was so easy for her to love people, her real estate career was next to none. People trusted her and loved her. And they bought property from her instead of the other ladies in the real estate company for which she worked.

I loved watching her close deals and seeing how people were so happy and content to be in her presence. Some even came back after their purchase with gifts and kind words. My mama was always grateful to have people like that in her life, even if it was only for a short time.

But through word of mouth, my mama was always busy selling homes. Families of previous buyers frequently sought her out. She was never idle, despite a few economic downturns we had during those times. She was always busy.

Despite all this, I don't think my mama felt confident around other people. She was an immigrant, and she always felt as if others were better than she, despite the fact that she was clearly better than a lot of people who were Canadian.

Fast-forward quite a few decades, and I, too, love to help people. I volunteer and love unconditionally everyone I meet, even people who are hard to love. Unfortunately, I've been taken advantage of over the years. But I still want to remain true to my upbringing and my mama's wonderful example of how to act towards others.

My mama was also a religious lady. She loved going to church. But she was equally happy worshipping in her own way at home. She created a makeshift altar with a statue of the Virgin Mary, St. Joseph, and St. Anne. We also had statues of St. Francis and St. Thérèse of Lisieux. The crucifix was in the center. Scattered around these statues and crucifix, she had candles. It was gorgeous.

Before meals, we joined hands and prayed in front of our altar, thanking God for all the food from his bounty. And we were grateful for all that God did for us. It was a wonderful moment celebration that brought us together every day before dinner on weekdays and on the weekends.

We also went to church on the weekends when we could and if my tata was home. He was an out-of-town construction worker, and there were times my mama and I were at home without him for weeks. But he loved his job, and he was glad when he was hired by a large construction company.

During these times, I felt so close to my mama. We cooked, sewed, washed clothes, cleaned the house (my mama was quite clean and fussy), and ironed clothes. I remember washing and ironing for hours. She changed the beds every week, and we even ironed the sheets and pillowcases.

Fast-forward many decades later, and my husband often mentions how hard I work to keep the house clean and tidy. I'm fussy too, but nothing like my mother, especially now as I am getting older. I have a few chronic conditions, so I don't have a lot of energy some days.

But what's even more momentous about those times when I was alone with my mama is how we used to just sit and talk together for hours. We didn't do a lot of TV watching during those days. We were lucky if we had two or three stations. And many of the shows were repeats. So spending time together became something we did a lot.

My mama was a beautiful lady. Well, what daughter wouldn't think her mother was beautiful, huh? But, growing up, I so wanted to be like her. Her face was always glowing and gorgeous. She dressed beautifully. Even when she stayed home, she put on a pretty blouse and a clean pair of slacks that matched her blouse. Her hair was always combed and styled. She just looked so beautiful.

Summer holidays were wonderful times too. I couldn't wait to get out of school so I could spend time with my mama. She knew how to rest, not just work.

We had a family cottage about 200 miles north of our home, in the eastern townships of Montreal, and we'd go there for weeks on end during the summer. The countryside around our cottage was so quiet. I remember taking my books and journals and just sitting or lying down on my lounger outside on nice days and doing nothing for hours. I loved these times and found them so deeply restorative.

My tata fished, and my mama fried the fish he caught. We ate fish a lot when we were at the cottage. But my mama also baked and cooked other things nonstop. That was one of the things we did together. I just loved to spend those times with my mama.

Cooking at the cottage was different. Our stove and oven weren't as powerful. But we still used them to cook and bake. And mama still made such wonderful pies and cakes. I always put on weight when we were at the cottage, despite the fact that I did a lot of walking.

But as August 1 approached, I started looking forward to going back to school. My mama always sewed me a new dress to wear the first day of the new school year. She'd start making it at the cottage, and then when we returned to the city around August 15, she'd put on the finishing touches.

Going back to school was always a wonderful time for me. I loved studying and doing well at school. I loved the library and was looking forward to meeting all my new teachers. But, more than that, there was something about just going to school that really appealed to me. I just loved to learn, to read, and to check out books from the library.

As I opened the door to my house when I came home from school, my mama ran to the door, gave me a great big hug, and kissed me. Aromas from my mama's cooking wafted through the house because she usually started prepping for dinner many hours before I came home. Sometimes, she used a Crock-Pot on the counter. It didn't matter what or how she was cooking, the house always smelled heavenly when I got home from school.

Then as I came into the kitchen, I usually saw a cake, some strudel, or some other delicious dessert on the counter. It was usually piping hot. Mama must have made it a half hour before she knew I would return from school. The house was so warm and inviting. It was such a wonderful time for me.

On any given night, I came home from school, got into my home clothes, and did my homework while my mama made supper. My mama always brought into my room a slice of homemade torte, strudel, or some of whatever she had made that afternoon so that I could continue studying until supper.

Then when it was time for supper, I ate my dinner with Mama and returned to my room to continue my homework or get into the comfy chair and read for an hour or two before going to bed. I had a lot of homework; this was back in the days when teachers believed in loading up the students with a lot to prepare for the next day. There were a lot of tests and quizzes too.

I'll never forget the day I heard that my grandmother passed away. I was twelve years old. I came home from school and knew right away something was very wrong. My mama's face was red, and her eyes were swollen, as if she had been crying for hours. She was sitting on the sofa, motionless. Typically, at that particular time of day, my mama would be running around doing so much to prepare for dinner. But that day was different.

As I came into the living room, I asked my mama if everything was okay. She said no. Then she told me that my grandmother had died the previous night.

I had never met my grandmother, as she lived in Kiev, but I had heard so much about her. My mama shared a story about her each week after Sunday dinner. When the Second World War broke out, my Mama was forced to leave her mama and her whole family. She never saw her mama again. So my grandmother's death really hit my mama hard.

As my mama sat crying, I wondered how I could help her commemorate and honor my grandmother's life from far away. We couldn't go back to Kiev. It was too late, and the funeral was the next day. As I sat beside my mama trying to comfort her, I wanted to create a space in our home that would both comfort my mama and honor my grandmother's life.

I didn't know how to talk to my mama about this because she was so upset. But as the days passed by, I decided to try to create a makeshift altar, one that was similar to the one my grandmother had in her home; I had seen it in the photos my mama shared with me over the years. I recalled there were always flowers, a few religious statues, a crucifix, incense, candles, and holy water.

Then, one day, while my mama was away, I started to assemble the items. I found in the basement a small table we weren't using. I cleaned it, put a pretty floral cloth over it, and placed a crucifix on it. I gathered a few candles and a bouquet of artificial flowers that were in a box in the basement. I also took one of the two statues I had of the Virgin Mary in my room and some incense, as well as some holy water I had in a small flask that I had brought home from church a while back.

Before my mama came home, I put all the items on the small table and arranged them in a circular fashion with the crucifix in the center. I also lit a few candles on either side of the crucifix and statue. It felt so real to me.

As I knelt to pray in front of this table, tears started flowing from my eyes. I knew in that moment my grandmother was watching over me as I prayed. I felt so connected to her. I prayed that my mama would feel some comfort in this sacred space, which was tucked into a corner of our living room.

When my mama came home, I greeted her at the door. I took her by the hand and led her to the small table in the corner of our living room.

She was visibly moved that I would create an altar to celebrate my grandmother's life. As she knelt in front of the little table, I joined her. We prayed for a few minutes in silence. And, somehow, the healing began. Right then, I felt connected to my mama and grandmother.

I've always believed that religion is a living component of our lives. Catholics certainly believe this when we are invited to live as disciples of God. This was one way for me to bring the living experience of religion into my home. I have continued to do that even now.

When my mama passed away in 2011, I was devastated. I had no idea how I was going to carry on. I had lost one of the most important and central people in my life. It was as if a part of me died with her. I wanted to create a way of honoring her life. So I thought about creating a home altar to honor her legacy and memory, just as I did when my mama's mother passed away.

I pondered for a while how I was going to accomplish creating this altar. Then I decided to plant a purple peony and create a makeshift altar in my backyard. My mama's favorite flowers were always purple peonies. She was also an avid lover of nature and found great comfort in communing with it. She always said that she saw God's handiwork in nature. She used to walk in the Botanical Gardens every day well into her eighties.

To honor my mother's life and who she truly was as a person, I devoted the left corner of my backyard to celebrating her life. I tilled the soil and added some fresh topsoil. That represented new beginnings for me. Just the process of creating this flower garden comforted me and helped me honor this wonderful lady whom I never want to forget.

Beside the purple peony, I made a cross from tree branches. Around the plant and cross, I planted a rose of Sharon bush and several hydrangea bushes. I also bought a small waterfall and placed that to the side of the bushes. This symbolized letting go, cleansing, and the continuous flow of energy and life. I wanted to create a space that reflected all things that my mama celebrated and drew energy from while she was alive. This way, I would be constantly reminded of her when I went into my backyard.

Over the years, this space has given me so much comfort. Every time I go into my backyard, I am still reminded of her in those beautiful purple peonies and the refreshing waterfall. I also put a small wooden chair beside it so I can sit down and say a few prayers.

But, more than that, I feel her presence somehow in that beautiful space. My mama would love it if she saw it. And this living symbol has helped me come to terms with her death. I realized that I didn't need to attend a church to get this feeling of completion and comfort or to honor her life.

My mama was one of the most wonderful people in my life. I look a lot like her, and I even act like her. I guess that shouldn't be surprising, given that I am her daughter and I spent so much time with her. But part of me feels connected with my mom, even now.

I miss her a lot, especially in the summer. But I have the makeshift memorial, and every summer I have beautiful flowers around it. It is a way of celebrating her, even now, a full decade since she passed away.

I love you, Mama, and I always will!
Your Doci!

This painting is a fragment of the dream that triggered my change through art. I named it Harvest.

Painting, Healing, and Having Faith

Let us inspire those who are afraid, not because we are brave, but because we have faith

Monica Septimio

Storyteller

I am the granddaughter of a wonderful woman. My paternal grandmother was a true Amazon, except she was five foot five and Northeastern Brazilian. She was brave; for example, when I saw her chopping off poisonous-snakes' heads with an axe, dropping her head to one side while the rest of her body writhed to the other. She was fearless. A super-artistic woman, she created, from scraps of cloth, beautiful blankets, rugs, and pillows of all the styles you can imagine. She was so ingenious that she went from raising chickens to pigs, from pigs to cows, and from cows to buying her own farm. No, it wasn't just her—my grandfather was the same way.

They could barely read. However, their wisdom and will-power made them reach beyond their dreams. Nothing was impossible for them; no problem impeded what they decided to do. My grandfather was a dreamer. When he told us something he was going to do, it usually seemed absurd to us. But even if it took a while, he carried out his project successfully.

From my grandparents, I learned how to love, to be obstinate, to be committed to fulfilling my dreams, and, of course, to tell stories. I believed that if I wanted something, and God did not object, I *would* accomplish whatever it was. In my teens, we installed electricity on my grandparents' farm. During my childhood, my family used kerosene lamps, so each morning my nostrils had to be cleaned, as they were undoubtedly black.

The most beautiful memories of my childhood are of my two grandparents. Before we went to sleep, my youngest aunt, who was four years older than I, sat with me as we listened to my grandparents' tales. It was like a ritual, and I couldn't wait until that magical moment when my grandmother told old wives' tales. At bedtime, she told us almost all the ancient fables in her own words. Today, I wonder how a semi-illiterate person knew so much about these stories, from the lying boy named Pinocchio, to the little girl who wore a red hood, to three little pigs building a house, and so on. But my favorite story was "Beauty and the Beast," followed closely by "Cinderella."

When I traveled, I pretended to be the characters in all those stories. When all the lights were off, and I was asleep, I dreamed of everything my grandmother told me. And for the stories that I didn't like the endings of, I invented my own happy endings. I have traveled in those tales narrated by my grandmother.

My grandmother also loved to tell the Brazilian folklore that was passed down from her ancestors. Some those stories scared me, and I imagined different conclusions—I always saved the day.

My grandfather told authentic and more elaborate chronicles of the past, narratives that he lived or heard about throughout his life. Some came from his genealogy, some stories were from the Bible, some were tales of saints who performed miracles, and some came from his own travels and exploits.

When I analyze this desire to tell stories, I realize that my initial spark to do the same came from those precious nights. If I struggled to sleep, I embarked on imaginary travels in the stories my grandparents had told. When I wanted to forget about some frustrations, I made up stories in my mind, which felt as if I were running away from reality when I was alone.

At my kindergarten graduation, I won my first book after learning to read. *The Legend of Alvorado* was about a wild white horse that helped other horses. As a teenager, I loved acting and found it easy to write plays. I didn't know how much I should do academically, but my creative ability to make up stories was very good. I also inherited from my mother her curiosity in exploring books and her love of writing.

With what seemed like suddenness, I grew up to the musicality of my father singing *vaquejada* (a sport typical of the Nordeste region of Brazil) tunes, which are musicalized tales about the fearless cowboys of Northeastern Brazil and the simplicity of life in that region. His deep, harmonious voice is still in my mind, helping me with the rhymes. That style of music is called *repente* or *aboio*—it's improvised, spontaneous music with unscripted rhymes created about a theme of the singers' choice. It's known for the fluid alignment of words in sentences and the passion in the message told as parables and metaphors. The cordel booklets—inexpensive leaflets that contain Brazilian folklore, poems, and songs—that came with us to Pará in Northeastern Brazil were a significant influence on my poetic side and on my desire to live a full and meaningful life.

Now, my proud father resurrects memories of his youthful adventures, suddenly enchanting friends with his smooth, rich voice when meeting. But I lost the other three. My grandparents lived full lives and died, leaving behind their beautiful story that marks their time here on earth; they are loved now as they were when alive. My mother rested in the Lord in 2020 due to complications after contracting COVID-19. She also reached her milestone before leaving us—she lived to see her daughters succeed and even her grandchildren achieve great goals. All four had notable lives, and all past hurts are forgiven, I choose to only remember the great examples of overcoming adversity, of wisdom, and of the love that they gave me. However, like my grandmother, I am only a storyteller, and my tale isn't about my four rocks.

Abandonment

This tale begins with the abandonment of a two-month-old child by his teenage mother when she felt preoccupied about being a minority and lacking experience. Living with her baby's father's parents' family and away from her own family, she freaked out and left her daughter in the care of her paternal grandparents. Her daughter's father was on a trip, and when he returned, he didn't find his then partner and mother of his daughter. At that moment, he went from thinking he had a family, to having a daughter without her mother.

Perhaps, this would be the moment when he began to take on the responsibility of a husband and family man. Who knows? Everything might have been different with a little more effort from this girl. But for one reason or another, in her despair, she left. Never knowing that her legacy she left behind for her baby was a future of emotional dysfunction and codependency.

Throughout her life, no matter how loved she was by her father, who played more of a brother's role in his daughter's life, she was completely centered on the shoulders of her grandparents, who loved her unconditionally. With all this zeal from her father and grandparents, that girl always felt that someone else must be the reason for her lack of happiness.

This is the first part of the story about my mother, my birth, and our misfortune. In my second month of life, my mother was insecure and unstable. She lived with my father in my paternal grandparents' house. According to her, my grandfather did not agree with this union. To make matters worse, some of my grandmother's relatives, out of great envy, wanted to take my mother's place.

With all the pressure and lack of support, she had to leave the house at the age of just nineteen. The arrangement was for her to settle down a little in life and then come back to get me. After four years she came back, and my grandparents didn't want to give me to her anymore. They had already fallen in love with the baby who was once given into their care by force. They ended up going to court to fight for custody of me. They won. My mother lost.

I didn't understand anything at the time. I just felt over the years the crater that abandonment makes. No matter the circumstances, those who have been abandoned suffer something that will cause a lot of damage. Most mothers don't leave their children because they don't love them or don't want the responsibility. Unfortunately, they leave because of something they think they can fix. Then, they come back hoping that the world stopped, and everything will be as it was when they left. But nothing stays the same. Every minute that passed, everything continued in motion, just like people's minds. What was once hard to find is now completely lost.

Unfortunately, for me, the first few months of a baby's life are when the bond between the mother and baby is created and formed for life. The misfortunes that both my mother and I suffered will be paid for over a lifetime. As much as I told my mom that I was okay and that I was where I had to be, as much as I had forgiven her for having to choose to leave me in a better place, she never stopped feeling pain.

I felt that pain when I made the same decision to leave my son behind, in my own country, to come to the United States. Before, I couldn't even approach the subject without getting hurt or angry, but once you're healed from a trauma, it doesn't hurt anymore. Yes, this is my tale.

Healing

The child does not stop loving his parents, but he stops loving himself, feeling unworthy of being loved, as if he were trash whom no one wants. The biggest problem with abandonment is the eternal feeling of emptiness. The eternal search to fill this void creates emotionally unstable people who are eternally needy and searching for a feeling that never fills them.

The worst period during this situation is adolescence. Adolescence for everyone is the most difficult time in their lives, as it is when they are searching for their own identities. Imagine, then, how difficult adolescence must be for those who no longer have any identity in the family with which they live.

My solution was a desire to be free from this void. And my healing came from my paintings, my therapy, and, of course, my God.

During my childhood, I had the stability of a family who loved me and of my mother who, whenever she could, came to visit me. She brought gifts and took me out with her as much as she could. Still, the early abandonment left ingrained consequences. How painful it is to be someone who was discarded from the life of the person who was the first to bond with you. I thought this was not a problem because I was loved from all sides—my grandparents, my father, and my uncles made sure that

I was protected and loved. Whenever my mother had the opportunity, she introduced me to members of her family too; some I am still in contact with. I thought the abandonment didn't negatively affect me, but unconsciously I developed a feeling that stayed with me for over forty years.

Not because it's my mother's fault, but because each chapter of life brings a sequence dependent on it, feelings that I had to identify and eliminate. But the biggest problem is, when these feelings become habits, they go unnoticed because they are old companions. Such habits acquired by small and large wounds in the soul, which were inflicted without treatment or attention, become chronic and affect your personality. These wounds cause you to act in ways that you think are just characteristic of you. My rebellion, resentment, envy of those who lived with both parents, desire to have a standard family, desire to have this emptiness filled, and desire to obtain what I think is missing—all these things seemed like common teenage angst. We all want what we don't have. But some only want what someone else has; once they get that or something similar, it no longer has any value.

Throughout my life, like a magnet, I have always been attracted to emotionally dependent people, to those like me, a codependent on a mission to "help." In this "help" I increasingly sank deeper into myself. I was forced to live the other person's life and to seek to achieve the dreams of the partner in question. I never allowed myself to have a dream of my own. In my last troubled, codependent relationship, which lasted fourteen years, it was clear from the beginning that he was not well. But the codependent goes through countless stages of denial to keep the object of codependency.

My ex-husband repeated the fallacy that "we must learn to be happy alone, because the company of others will be a matter of choice, not necessity." He said this to remind me that I was always a necessity to him. I was never his first choice. I was someone who helped him when no one was there, who picked him up when he was down. I wasn't someone he wanted and had chosen to grow old by his side. I was a necessity, the self-effacing codependent for the emotionally dependent.

I learned a lot from this, but I only put it into practice after almost fourteen years, after hearing him repeat it many times. Stupid people hide behind excuses to continue in their vicious cycle because both making decisions and making them happen are very painful. So I lived blindly because I refused to see what was clearly before my eyes. In this blindness, I insisted on guiding another person who was also blind, as they still had a shadow over their development and unconscious traumas from their childhood. Of course, it was already clear that this relationship was not going to work.

And so it happened, between betrayals and forgivenesses, which is what happens in the middle of a relationship like this; one acts by taking advantage of the codependent's unconditional commitment, and the other doesn't care about anything other than feeling good. These acts by an emotionally unbalanced person to feel good range from lying to supporting the codependent, and then temporary regret followed by another lie to the codependent who will certainly believe it. This cycle will repeat as long as it is allowed or until the emotionally unbalanced person finds another codependent who appears to be more attractive.

The codependent goes unnoticed because he is strong and always sees that the other remains emotionally weak while the codependent sinks, disappearing within himself. When the object of codependency is taken away by death or abandonment, the codependent no longer has anything, not even their own life, because they lived for the other. He dreamed other people's dreams; he never grew up because he was the shadow of the other person he made grow while the codependent stayed still.

Excessive dependence on others often leads to dysfunctional interpersonal relationships. The person on whom the codependent depends is a person who will forgive and blame the actions, not the person, for the harm that is inflicted, similar to the case of a mother whose son is addicted to drugs, is sick, or has some type of disorder.

A metaphor that I use in my painting groups is about the empty vase or container. Throughout our lives, we fill ourselves with knowledge, experiences, and traumas. Like a vase, we can be clean or stained. Like a vase, we can be broken. Like a vase, we can be full of both good and bad things. The vase must be maintained; the things that are acquired and that should not be retained must be cleaned away. Everything that could cause damage to the vase must be removed. But if this maintenance is not carried out, the items in the vase can rot and die, and the vase itself can be indelibly stained and damaged.

The codependent is a vessel that, due to lack of maintenance, always absorbs and compromises. Codependency is acquired not only by the current state of life, but by a series of factors that in the past overloaded the vessel. The codependent vessel is low in maintenance and therefore vulnerable to being what it is. This emotional deficiency is not caused by a single relationship. Codependency is a vessel that has become emotionally affected since childhood.

Codependency is a behavior that disguises itself and goes unnoticed, but it is a disorder of emotions. I needed to know that I had to seek help. Many end up putting up with everything to save their marriages or loved ones, until they end up getting sick too.

Change requires confrontation. Confrontation requires a decision. The decision, in turn, will only flow with attitudes.

Trauma causes unbalanced emotions. Unbalanced emotions end up making you look for wrong ways to get some personal satisfaction; it is a continuous silence that annuls you.

The probability of change is completely remote. There has to be some struggle forcing you into the unwanted transition of change. Otherwise, you would go into a deep, dark hole, and the more time that passes, the more decayed you would become.

The break is the same for many, but some have the resilience to be emotionally reborn. Others, unfortunately, will die. And be reborn.

Metamorphosis

On August 25, 2014, I dreamed that I was at my grandparents' house in my hometown. I was packing my personal things for a permanent move. So I started putting my things in boxes. They weren't just suitcases, but boxes for a big move. I came across a beautiful, shapely, thin wooden shelf.

In a dream, I saw a man wearing a cloak of peace, as if he was someone illustrious. Wherever he passed, people's faces changed to a singular expression—peace.

In the place where I lived as a child, he was sitting at a table. In his hand, a pen like a gold, it seemed of great value. He wrote on a blank sheet of paper. I couldn't read what he wrote, as it wasn't a language I knew; however, I could understand that he was giving me a mission to fulfill. When I was ready, he wrote an order.

I stopped in front of a wooden shelf, on it items had already been arranged in many organized boxes. I saw a lot of shoes on that shelf, shoes from my childhood that my innocent little feet had used. I recognized other shoes that I wore throughout my life and shoes that I still don't have, representing the dispersed past and a prepared future.

On the last shelf, there are sandals made with leather and blue beads, a spotlight on them from the lamp at the top of the shelf. I knew they were the most important thing I would wear, but, somehow, I knew my feet weren't ready to wear them. I knew that shoes mean preparation, and I was being prepared for a project that I still had no idea what it was.

I packed everything I needed to put in boxes. I took the paper from the man's hands. Even without seeing his face, his smile spread glory over me.

I woke up and went to work. When I arrived, I somehow needed to mark the dream. My stepdaughter had three colors of paint, two brushes, and two canvases left over from a school project. I started my first canvas and haven't stopped until today.

I had forgotten about all that. I didn't even imagine returning to my roots in my adult phase. I never dreamed of what I'm living now. For more than forty years, I never thought about being an artist, but my blood held my artistic heritage. I didn't know that my creative streak would influence my healing. However, God knew. He made my whole heritage clear through a dream. Activated art became healing!

Moreover, I didn't know how to do anything. I had to learn from scratch. The art worked to cure me. It branched out in countless directions and transformed my life, starting to put on a canvas my emotions, both those that make me feel inadequate and those that make me feel worthy, and especially my dreams.

For many long years, I remained motionless in the corner of the board, similar to a queen held by horses in a chess game. At forty-one years old, I was already in the middle of a game in which the queen is not expected to move. The game of chess seemed over, and God urged the queen to start a new round.

Art through painting, and then later through writing, took me out of the shadows and gave me an identity, made me look inside myself and analyze what should be balanced. I could only bring out through painting what was within my personal shadow, as if I poured it onto the canvas. I didn't understand what was happening. I didn't know the power of art as a cure; however, it was happening to me.

During this latent period, of which I now have much more understanding, I surrendered. Everything I did was an essential tool for healing my wounded soul, but I had no idea at the time; I just felt it. I needed a refuge to ease my pain, and painting was that refuge. I wasn't inspired by any artist or friends, nor did I get any tips from anyone. I never had the inclination to seek help from art. All of this really happened overnight and was a turning point in my life. Certainly, in my original form, I was created to be what I am today, but I was hidden and came to light in my moment of darkness.

Art has a power beyond our physical capabilities; it syncs with the subconscious. Art reveals what consciously would be impossible to express. Unconscious synergy and art make the projection of the unknown possible. Art, with its delicacy, takes not only the best, but also the worst of me and exposes it without causing pain. On the contrary, it helps, giving possibilities to clarify what cannot be said, but rather expressed through art.

Psychology and neuroscience would certainly say that it was all my psychic energy that strongly projected my artistic side in the midst of the crisis to save me. My subconscious brought the help I needed from my original form. In my faith, I am sure that what I experienced was a gift from my God to transform my life.

Convinced that what I experienced with art as a cure worked in practice, I decided to go back to college to learn the theory of what I experienced; it is still slow going. To me, God is the chief psychologist; He used my dreams to direct me. He instructed me how to get the message I dreamed of and helped me so much by guiding me towards what I was experiencing. After ten years of this death, mourning came, and the mourning expressed by paints and canvases, in turn, gave life to more than six hundred canvases, six books, coauthorship in three anthologies, and countless art exhibitions.

Loss breaks and can even kill. God transformed the silence of death into art and art into life. Since *Shattered Silence* transformed into artwork, it has inspired people both near and far, even in different countries.

We wait for miracles, forgetting that every day we are living in one.

In Memory of
Angelina Umina

Beyond Words

A Love-Letter Legacy
Written by My Grandmother

Lisa Michelle Umina

My grandmother, Angelina, began a new chapter in her life shortly after I was born, when she moved to California to live with her sister Emma and settled into a small apartment. I'm not sure why she made this decision. She lived far away from her two sons and her four grandchildren, who were all in Cleveland. She nurtured her connection with distant loved ones by consistently sending heartfelt letters through the mail, a gesture that holds a unique significance in today's vastly changed landscape.

In retrospect, our geographical differences didn't weaken our bond. When I went to see my great-grandmother

Mary, she always planned a ritual. I used to sit at the dining room table with blue sheets of paper, pencil, and eraser she stored in her antique hutch. I remember it took me hours to write a two-page letter. Over the years, our written exchanges persisted, and a significant change unfolded when my grandmother returned to Cleveland following the passing of her mother.

In the quiet embrace of memories, I find myself drawn to the essence of my beloved grandmother, a guardian of love. As I begin to write our journey of words, it is not just a narrative about her, but a tribute to the unwavering love that formed the very fabric of who I am. My grandma had a particular way of expressing her love, a love that may have been difficult at times. Nonetheless, from time to time, she surprised me with a little trinket or sacred prayer book from the shrine where her charitable heart resided.

I know that there are numerous love tales, but the bond I shared with my grandma was special and meaningful. She stands out as a glowing exemplar of that distinct brand of affection when I reflect on those who imparted lessons about love. In the tapestry of my life, the threads woven with my grandmother stand out as vibrant and irreplaceable. Every visit to her home was an experience filled with love and warmth, her cozy home elevated by the little details. She added more than mere time to the hours we spent together; we had so many conversations about everything and anything.

She had an uncanny ability to look out for me. I recall a specific instance when my first book was featured in the newspaper, and she expressed her immense pride. Yet, amid her compliments, she insisted my front tooth was crooked, and I needed braces, especially if I intended to be in the newspapers or anywhere in public again promoting my book. It was her unique way of showing love, and I understood her underlying intention.

She had a remarkable way with words, I must say. Her affect and comments seemed harsh sometimes, but I could always tell that she didn't mean any harm. Some family members and her friends, however, found it difficult to interpret her remarks or sarcasm as well-intentioned. I often found myself in the position of apologizing on her behalf.

My grandmother's kitchen always smelled of garlic, even if she wasn't cooking. Even today, when I am cooking and I use garlic, I immediately think of her. Her lunches were more than just meals; they were carefully cooked and presented on pretty dishes, the table dressed with embroidered napkins.

Each visit, she brought me a present as a sign of her love. It may be a treasured memento from her life, a necklace that whispered stories from her past, or a thoughtfully selected item she knew would make me happy. These treasures were more than just gifts; they were physical representations of our relationship and acts of love.

Thinking back on such moments, with those gifts, I see that my grandma was teaching me how to make treasured memories out of the ordinary fabric of life. But even more than the delicious food and tangible presents, it was my grandmother's considerateness that enriched our experiences. What remains most vivid in my memory is her ability to transform everyday letters into treasured works of art, infusing them with a touch of artistry that made them genuinely extraordinary.

She adorned each handwritten card with gorgeous cutouts of tiny girls whirling in pastel-colored skirts and angels with golden wings. Her timeworn hands, with subtle grace, masterfully created each piece. Her artistic talent was also visible on the envelopes, which were adorned with these whimsical images that danced around the edges, setting the stage for the moving words that were inside. These precious scraps of paper developed a language all their own and conveyed tales of warmth, compassion, and affection.

Every envelope opened like a gift, unveiling a realm where love found expression through carefully selected words and charming paper cutouts, often sourced from magazines or newspapers. On the backs of the envelopes, she always added "S.W.A.B.K." *Sealed with a big kiss.*

Over the course of thirty-five years, the collection of letters grew, a tribute to a lifetime of shared memories.

Each cutout had meaning—a heart, a little girl, the Blessed Mother, angels. I can remember each one as if she wrote it yesterday. Even now, as I read those precious letters, the angels and young girls continue to remind me of the countless hours she spent making each letter or card.

When I made the big move to Mexico, it broke my heart that my weekly trips to my grandmother's house would turn into yearly visits, or sometimes twice a year. It never seemed as if it were enough time with her, and I couldn't stay long because she needed to lie down to rest in the afternoons. She had become more fragile each time I came to visit her.

My grandmother continued to write me when I moved to Mexico. She complained every time about the long Mexican address. I completely understand; it is a very long address, and the layout of the street address is different. I can honestly say I do not receive much mail here because of this, not to mention the turnaround time can take up to three to four months to receive a letter from anywhere in the world. God love her for trying. I could often see that she had attempted to address the missive correctly, but instead of organizing the lines properly, she scratched off some words and added others. I started to notice the cutouts were fewer and fewer.

The last letter that arrived, before she was too weak to write, was plain and simple—no ornate cutouts of angels or hearts. I opened the letter, and there it was, a masterpiece of exhaustion. "Dearest Lisa," it began, "I had such a hard time writing your long address out on the envelope that I am too damn tired to write you a letter and sign it. I love you, Grandma." Now, most people would stash the envelope for a fresh start the next day, but not my grandmother. Oh no, this was her way of saying, "You live too damn far, and I'm just plain exhausted."

My grandma had strange habits and peculiarities, yet her love was a strong influence in my life. She had a way of contrasting her love of vivid words with the innate tenderness she displayed in her daily routines. She got up at four in the morning and spent her time saying rosaries and novenas in fervent prayer for her friends and family. Although her outward appearance suggested toughness, she concealed a tenderness that she rarely displayed. Few knew about her vulnerable side because she tended to guard her emotions well. My father used to talk about how hard she was on him, which I could see in action when we visited. Her stubborn walls baffled me, especially considering how obvious her love was for my father. I was confused by the contrast between her tough demeanor and her obvious affection for him.

A piece of my grandmother seemed to go with my father when he passed away. Her eyes lost their brightness. It was then that I realized, behind that thick wall of hers, a part of her died with him. That's when I started to wonder why some parents have a hard time showing their kids how much they truly love them. Yet, when it is their grandchildren, they do not have any reservations. My grandmother had her own way of showing love, but I wanted my father to see the tender side of her. I think he did when he saw his mother and me together.

The hardest part of saying goodbye to my grandma was the physical barrier that divided us in her last moments. I knew she didn't want me to see her fading, and she issued a "no visitors" order, permitting only medical workers to attend her. I am filled with an immense gratitude that words cannot fully capture for my cousin Nikki, who stealthily checked on her.

With his nurse's uniform on, Kyle managed to elude the nurses and set up a FaceTime call, which allowed me to be virtually present for those brief final moments with my grandma. I felt an intense pain upon her death, one that was comparable to losing the love of my life. The distance that stood between us at that critical moment added to the grief and intensified the anguish. I cannot fathom what I would have done if I couldn't say goodbye to her.

The influence of my grandma is still very much present and has braided itself into the core of who I am. Even though I didn't start the journey of parenthood myself, her love lessons have served as my compass, helping me navigate the complex world of relationships. My grandma

Angelina was a master of love; the smallest elements made up her symphony. She taught me the language of love, which is expressed in little, nuanced details, rather than in large, dramatic actions. For me, the art of love became a string of well-chosen phrases, memorable dinners, and unplanned gestures of love.

The value of expressing love in writing was one of the lessons that stuck with me the most. I picked up a pen and wrote some love notes to myself, motivated by the letters my grandmother had written me. These romantic letters developed into a link between hearts, an eternal communication that surpasses the transient quality of spoken words. The handwritten letter is a monument to the lasting power of concrete, unique gestures of love in this age of digital communication.

I also developed a love for cooking. The attention I give to the details in planning and preparing a meal has also become a way to show my affection for the people I love. More than just food, it is a way of expressing, "You matter, and this is my gift to you."

Thinking back on these teachings, I see that love is found in the little things, the nuanced details that come together to form a beautiful symphony of love. It's about the happiness of an unexpected gift, the scent of a well-prepared dinner, and the coziness of a handwritten note. These are the little things that make the ordinary remarkable.

My grandma showed me that love's beauty may be found in the small things, even in a world that is sometimes enthralled with spectacular displays. It is not the expensive presents or grandiose acts that leave an impression on the heart; rather, it's the small, everyday things that get ingrained in memories. Caring involves taking the time to attend to small details. It's crucial to show the people you care about that you've invested the effort in these thoughtful acts. Life is in the details, my grandmother used to tell me. It's in how we treat the individuals who are important to us. It's in the work we do to ensure they feel noticed, appreciated, and loved. We run the danger of missing a crucial piece in the intricate fabric of life when we ignore the little things.

All in all, my grandmother left me a love legacy presented in words that were precise. With this insight, I find myself navigating the currents of life and understanding that love is expressed not only by grandiose pronouncements, but also by the nuanced strokes of little, day-to-day deeds. The small things—the kind notes, the homemade meals, the unexpected gifts—are what accentuate the route of love and add significance to the experience. Ultimately, a timeless love story is woven from the small elements, the subtle intricacies.

I kept all my grandmother's letters in a wonderful handmade Mexican box. Periodically, I open the box, close my eyes, and take in the memories that each letter holds, each as it was given to me. Every line demonstrates her knowledge and sense of humor. The thing I adore the most is that each envelope opens to show me pages of her conversing with me as though we were having lunch in her kitchen.

I've been thinking about how important it is to honor my grandmother's great heart in my own deeds ever since she passed away. By being mindful of life's little details, I hope to uphold her legacy. I try to return the favor by showing my love through modest gestures and attentive details, just as her small acts of kindness moved me. The real grandeur of her character was revealed in her seemingly minor deeds. Making a phone call, sending a sincere text, or cooking a meal can all be considered small yet meaningful ways to show someone you care. I wish to continue her legacy by embracing the ability of little, meaningful gestures to remind others that they are appreciated, as I am aware of the enormous influence these acts had on me.

I notice that I often adopt her mannerisms in my everyday interactions with those around me. I'm aware that the small gestures I extend to others are aimed at making them feel valued and remembered. In our contemporary world, where communication is dominated by cell phones and text messages, genuine and thoughtful gestures seem to be scarce or nonexistent.

In emulating my grandmother's thoughtful acts, I strive to carry on her legacy of considering others in the smallest details. Her kindness has left an indelible mark on my approach to relationships and daily life. From the little gestures she made to ensure I felt special and cherished, I've learned the profound impact of thoughtfulness.

As I navigate the fast-paced world dominated by technology and fleeting interactions, I find solace in replicating her genuine care. Whether it's a handwritten note, a small gift, or a heartfelt gesture, I aim to uphold the tradition of making people feel seen and appreciated. In a society where personal connections often take a back seat to convenience, I draw inspiration from my grandmother's unwavering commitment to fostering meaningful relationships through the power of small, thoughtful actions.

My grandmother's influence continues to shape the way I engage with the world. I strive to perpetuate the warmth and connection she instilled in our relationship. I find purpose in upholding her legacy of genuine care and appreciation. Through simple yet meaningful gestures, I aim to make a positive impact on others, just as my grandmother did for me. In doing so, I hope to perpetuate a cycle of kindness and thoughtfulness that echoes her enduring spirit.

In the end, it's the little things, the details, that create a love story that transcends time.

About the Authors

https://franwalshward.com

The life of **Fran Walsh Ward, PhD,** has been an adventure. Like Ellyn (in her fantasy/metaphysical series *Travels with Ellyn and Beyond the Drawbridge*, (written using the pen name Frances Ellen Walsh), she has traveled a spiritual path. Following her heart, she is an author, artist, and educator. Passionate about everything she does and everywhere she goes, she shares her joy of living and interacting with members of our global family who all complement each other. Peace and harmony are underlying currents of her existence. Grateful for her experiences, she eagerly anticipates her next chapters of life as they are revealed to her and as she has described them in her memoir *Soul Tattoos!*

Anapaula Corral is a loved and highly respected professional in her community. She was born in Mexico City and raised in Switzerland. She has an accomplished thirty-year career in the hospitality and residential industries. Her interest in writing her first book came from helping families and women who have lost a child. Writing was a healing and life-changing process for her. She intends to inspire other readers by writing more books on building strong and healthy communities and relations. She currently resides in Miami, Florida, with her boyfriend, Darryl, and their two dogs. She enjoys living life to the fullest and cherishes Anasofia's life every day.

Angela Gilson was born and raised in California. She published her first book in November 2022, at the age of twenty-three. The book is called *Sarabeth and Her New Best Friend*, which she dedicated to her rabbit, Hopper. She is a nature person who loves the outdoors and likes to travel.

Conrad M. Gonzales is a retired San Antonio firefighter and paramedic. He lives in San Antonio, Texas, USA. He is also a musician, performer, and songwriter, talents which he discovered later in life. He is the embodiment of the belief that "It is never too late to do great things to make a difference." Mr. Gonzales's passion has always been to provide safety education in order to save lives, especially those of children. To that end, he has been teaching safety to both children and adults for over forty years. He often says, "Children are our future, and I want to do whatever I can so that they live to see their future." You can listen to Captain Conrad, the Singing Firefighter on his social media channel.

Dave Grunenwald is a proud grandfather who was born, raised, and educated in Northeast Ohio. He has worn many hats in his professional life. Now "semi-retired", Dave has been an influential real-estate developer and attorney in Northeast Ohio for the last 30+ years. While he is still involved and active in that capacity, much of his time these days is spent wearing his DCGifts hat, creating the *Grandparent Merit Badges*™ series, and authoring a new series of children's story books.

Diane Lopes is a mother, daughter, sister, friend, corporate executive/leader, animal lover, and cancer fighter. Diane's father, Jack, became an author in his retirement which sparked Diane's desire to write. Diane's grief journey began when Jack started showing signs of dementia and aphasia. It was a years-long process that was difficult, agonizing, and sad, but sometimes funny as the shenanigans spark that was always there between the two, would peek out occasionally.

Diane has a children's book coming out soon called *Meet Jack Joybubbles*, a story about her family's rescue dog. Look for that coming soon from Halo Publishing International.

www.drcarolmankes.com
drcarolmankes@gmail.com

Dr. Carol Leibovich-Mankes, DrOT, OTR/L, PLCC, GC-C, was born in Israel to Argentinian parents and later emigrated to the USA. She is a multilingual professional fluent in English, Spanish, and Hebrew. With a career spanning twenty-five years, she serves as a pediatric occupational therapist and parent coach specializing in empowering kids (ages three to eighteen), parents, and teachers of exceptional children; she offers guidance on parenting, learning, handwriting, and other challenges they may face as life happens.

As an expert in her field, Dr. Leibovich-Mankes has faced personal challenges, including being a widow and a solo mom navigating through various losses and life transitions. Leveraging her experiences and professional expertise as an occupational therapist, certified life/parent coach, and grief counselor, she has forged a path of healing. Dr. Leibovich-Mankes is dedicated to supporting others in similar circumstances, advocating for empowerment, and raising awareness about grief and loss. Through coaching, she encourages individuals to adopt a growth mindset and recognize that grief can manifest from different significant losses. These losses don't always encompass death but may also stem from loss of control, unexpected circumstances, and unique challenges posed by parenting exceptional children. These losses can greatly impact one's emotional well-being and ability to navigate life's challenges.

In addition to her clinical and coaching work, Dr. Leibovich-Mankes is the author of the book *On the Road to Handwriting Success: A Resource Guide for Therapists, Teachers, and Parents*. This comprehensive guide reflects her commitment to sharing knowledge and insights, in addition to offering practical support for individuals involved in the development of children's handwriting and learning skills.

With a heartfelt mission to inspire and empower others to face and overcome loss, pain, and shattered dreams, Dr. Leibovich-Mankes emphasizes the importance of understanding grief as a dynamic process applicable to various life experiences. Her goal is to ensure that society recognizes diverse forms of loss and grief, especially the emotional turmoil and myriad challenges that may be associated with raising an out-of-the-box child. Dr. Leibovich-Mankes stands ready to guide parents, siblings, teachers, caregivers, and, most of all, children toward a future filled with hope, laughter, and renewed vitality.

Irene S. Roth is a freelance writer and author. Ms. Roth was born in Montreal, but now lives in Ontario with her husband, Toby (cat), and Milo (dog). She writes self-help books for adults and the chronically ill. She uses her expertise in psychology and philosophy to educate people of all ages on how to live their most authentic and fulfilling lives. She also presents workshops for *Savvy Authors*.

Brazilian impressionist, artist, and author, **Monica Septimio** resides in Natick. She was healed and transformed by the power of art. Now, she pours her soul into art inspired by dreams, childhood, faith, and culture.

In 2015, during an obscure time of her life, after one dream she started painting. Self-taught, she delivers the message that art cures. She has impacted many who have attended her exhibitions. She is the author of four children's bilingual books and one for adult readers, *Joy*. She was a seminarian for four years at Community Preservation Committee in Framingham, Massachusetts. She studied philosophy for two years at the University of Philosophy of Maranhão, Rondon do Pará, Brazil. She is currently active in the Boston community and attends book fairs and conferences, in addition to exhibiting her paintings and promoting her literary pieces.

Award-Winning Author

Lisa Michelle Umina is the founder and CEO of Halo Publishing International, a company that has been in operation since 2002. She also established Hola Publishing Internacional as its sister company. Lisa, who is an award-winning author herself, provides coaching to fellow writers on publishing their own books and developing lucrative public speaking careers. She shares the tactics she has used to achieve success. Lisa is the author of the award-winning book "Milo and the Green Wagon," and the host of the "Award-Winning Authors" podcast.

YaleNewHaven Health
Smilow Cancer Hospital

At Smilow Cancer Hospital, they offer the utmost in cancer care excellence. Their affiliation with Yale Cancer Center, the only National Cancer Institute (NCI)-designated comprehensive cancer center in Connecticut and one of only 56 Centers in the nation, means patients receive top-tier collaboration.

This partnership brings together esteemed scientists and physicians from Yale Cancer Center, Yale School of Medicine, and Smilow Cancer Hospital, ensuring optimal strategies for cancer prevention, detection, diagnosis, and treatment.

They provide 13 specialized cancer programs, each backed by teams of experts deeply versed in specific cancer types. Placing patients and their loved ones at the heart of their commitment, their approach prioritizes compassion and support throughout every individual's unique journey.

Halo Publishing International is a hybrid publishing company that combines the best aspects of traditional publishing and self-publishing. Our company aims to provide a flexible and affordable publishing options for authors who want more control over the publishing process while still receiving professional editing, design, and global distribution services. Halo Publishing International offers a wide range of publishing packages and services to suit different author needs and budgets, including editorial services, cover design, book formatting, printing, distribution, and marketing. With a focus on quality, integrity, and innovation, Halo Publishing International has helped numerous authors achieve their publishing goals and reach a wider audience.

OUR HISTORY

Halo Publishing International, our mission is to empower authors to share their stories worldwide. Since 2002, we have helped thousands of authors turn their ideas into published books that reach audiences globally. No matter the genre, whether it be science fiction, religious, children's literature, or an instruction manual, Halo Publishing International is dedicated to providing the editorial support needed to make your book a success.

OUR MISSION

Halo Publishing International is a self-publishing company that publishes adult fiction and non-fiction, children's literature, self-help, spiritual, and faith-based books. We continually strive to help authors reach their publishing goals and provide many different services that help them do so.

We do not publish books that are deemed to be politically, religiously, or socially disrespectful, or books that are sexually provocative, including erotica.

Halo reserves the right to refuse publication of any manuscript if it is deemed not to be in line with our principles.

Follow us on our social media
HaloPublishingInternacional

To know more about Halo Publishing International please visit
www.halopublishing.com

Milton Keynes UK
Ingram Content Group UK Ltd.
UKHW051841210424
441487UK00005B/28